Peacemakers
The New Generation
A "How To" Guide

Practical Group Activities for Grades 6 through 8

Written by Mary Fox and Claire M. Perez • Illustrated by Maureen McLain

In memory of
Richie DeGrand
our "Littlest Peacemaker"

Scripture excerpts have been taken from Revised New Testament of *The New American Bible* Copyright 1986 Confraternity of Christian Doctrine, Inc., Washington, DC.

Used. with permission. All rights reserved. No part of *The New American Bible* may be reproduced by any means without permission in writing from the copyright owner, except for those excerpts found on page 9 of this text.

THE BOOK TEAM

Ernie Nedder, Publisher   Kathy Nedder, CFO   Rev. Thomas M. Santa, CSsR, Theological Consultant
Aztech Publishing Services, Design and Production Services

Additional copies of this publication may be purchased by sending check or money order for $19.95 plus $5.00 postage and handling to: E.T. NEDDER Publishing Warehouse, 1526 East 16th Street, Tucson, AZ 85701-2861. Or call toll free 1-877-817-2742. Fax: 1-520-798-1514. Email: sales@fillorders.com. Be sure to check our website for a list of other products: www.nedderpublishing.com.

ISBN 1-893757-32-3
10 9 8 7 6 5 4 3 2

PEACEMAKERS
The New Generation

Table of Contents

Acknowledgments

We are grateful for the lessons in communication skills and conflict resolution from the Grace Contrino Abrams Peace Education Foundation Inc., P.O. Box 19-1153, Miami Beach, FL, 33919.

We would like to thank all the young Peacemakers who piloted these activities at the day camps at St. Patrick's Catholic Church in St. Charles, IL and at the overnight summer program at Resurrection Center, Woodstock, IL. The counselors and staff at each of those programs gave us valuable input and support. Jay Fox has been there from the beginning with his assistance and expertise. To Yvonne Perez and Emma Jay Fox, two counselors who were our greatest help and our toughest critics, and to Molly Fox and David Perez, two special Peacemakers who have been our inspiration and motivation, we offer this book with love.

About the Authors

Mary Fox, MRE and Claire M. Perez, MRE, both mothers and educators, worked together to develop and direct a summer camp for training Peacemakers. Mary is a peace activist and a pre-school teacher in Crystal Lake, Illinois. Claire is the producer of *Faith Talks*, a talk show and *Religious Educators Training*, a program for training catechists both of which appear on local access public television in Aurora, Illinois. She is the Deanery Director of Religious Education in Aurora, Illinois.

Maureen McLain, MRE, artist, served as a counselor at *Peacemakers: The New Generation Day Camp* and directed a Peacemakers summer program at her parish. Maureen is the Director of Religious Education at Christ the King Parish in Wonder Lake, Illinois.

Peacemakers: The New Generation could not be timelier. In a culture that breeds violence, in a time when children are accustomed to feeling insecure and threatened, this book teaches our youth that love and justice and peace are attainable realities. By providing concrete examples, games, crafts and prayers Perez and Fox intentionally teach peacemaking in these critical times. The lessons in non-violent conflict resolution, cooperative living, understanding the world in which we live, and positive communication provide children with the tools they need to be effective Peacemakers.

— Bishop Tom Gumbleton

Introduction

Several years ago, disturbed by the amount of violence in our country and particularly devastated by the violent acts of children, we were forced to evaluate the situation. We realized that, as a society, we have unwittingly taught our children that violence is the norm. We have immersed them in violent language, surrounded them with violent images and modeled violent behavior. We inferred, that unless adults began to take responsibility for teaching them, our children would never learn how to successfully live in this world filled with conflict, or ever break out of the cycle of violence.

The time has come, we told each other, to be pro-active in reversing the trend toward violence. Adults must stop blaming one another for the trouble. Instead each of us must take responsibility for our own actions. If society has not purposely taught our children to be violent, certainly we have carelessly failed to teach them to be nonviolent. We asked ourselves, "How do we teach peaceful living to children in a chaotic society?"

Ghandi tells us that in order to understand nonviolence we must first recognize violence in our own lives. We started there, looking for the sources of violent behavior. We found that attitudes of arrogance and prejudice lead to injustice which can lead to violence. Ignorance and isolation foster injustice as well. Uncontrolled feelings of loneliness, fear and anger can generate inappropriate responses that can also lead to violence.

As parents and educators, we knew that we could give our children different models. We could show them their value and purpose in the world. We could remind them that, being Children of God, they are never alone. We could assure them that, because God loves all of us equally, they need never feel inferior or superior to anyone else. We could demonstrate how, being one family of God, we are all interrelated and responsible to one another.

In addition, we knew it would be important to give the children the skills to communicate effectively, to understand and manage anger and to resolve conflict peacefully. Finally we would name them "Peacemakers" giving them an identity as people of God who bring love into the world.

Peacemakers: The New Generation is a small step in that direction. It began as a day camp at St. Patrick Church in St. Charles, Illinois. We used familiar games and crafts and processed them with the specific purpose of teaching lessons in peacemaking. In addition, we designed new games, crafts and prayer services around such themes as self-identity, compassion, human dignity and forgiveness. We also created lesson plans for effective communication, cooperative living and nonviolent conflict resolution. Quiet time was set aside for reflection and journaling. In this idealistic environment everyone was allowed to participate in any activity. Games were non-competitive, so there were no losers. Bullying and put-downs were not allowed. If children slipped into these behaviors they were quickly and respectfully reminded of the expectations of Peacemakers.

Later we were invited to use our materials in a four-day, overnight summer program at Resurrection Center in Woodstock, Illinois. Each year, several groups of children from varied backgrounds and cultures gather from inner city Chicago and rural McHenry County to put our lessons to the test. Children leave with a better understanding of themselves, a deeper appreciation of the diversity in our world, and some skills for coping in a violent society. One young person told her mother as she walked to her car on the last day, "I'm feeling more peaceful already!"

It is our hope that you will find these activities catalysts for your work with children. It is important to note that the times given are estimates. Be creative in molding these plans to fit the needs of your children into the time frames of your programs. They have been used in junior high religion classes, as substitute for Vacation Bible School and as all day retreats and workshops. The possibilities are limitless. It is the way that each activity is processed that teaches the lesson. One idea will lead to another as you provide peaceful learning environments for the children in your lives.

We welcome your comments and suggestions. Our e-mail address is **Peacemakerstng@yahoo.com.** Best wishes in all your efforts. Peace!

— Claire and Mary

BEGINNING ACTIVITIES

*We begin with three activities that can be used at any time. They will enhance and unify the other activities presented throughout the book. The **Prayer of Saint Francis** is a traditional prayer for Peacemakers. The **Circle of Peace** can be the center of any program. Children look forward to gathering in a safe place for prayer and open discussion. It might begin or end every session. Suggestions for journaling will be presented at the end of each chapter. If you plan to use the journaling activities a special **Peacemakers Journal** may be appropriate.*

Prayer of Saint Francis   10 minutes (Pray the prayer often!)

Materials: Poster of prayer or prayer written out on sheets, music if you wish to sing it.
 Purpose: To pray for peace and the strength to be Peacemakers.

PRAYER OF SAINT FRANCIS

Lord make me an instrument of your peace,
Where there is hatred, let me sow love;
Where there is injury, pardon;
Where there is doubt, faith;
Where there is despair, hope;
Where there is darkness, light;
And where there is sadness, joy!
O divine Master, grant that I may not so much seek
To be consoled as to console,
To be understood as to understand,
To be loved as to love.
For it is in giving that we receive,
It is in pardoning that we are pardoned,
It is in dying that we are born to eternal life.

AMEN

Circle of Peace

Materials: (optional) Table with candles and Bible or other symbols, music.
 Purpose: To gather in a safe place for prayer and discussion.

Plan an aural cue such as music, a spoken phrase, a chime or a song that will always be used to gather the group into the *Circle of Peace.*

Gather the children in a circle, around the table, if you choose this option. Demonstrate the cue. Tell them that this is the signal to form a circle and quiet themselves. Explain that this is the *Circle of Peace* where respect will be shown to every member. In a circle no one is higher or lower, first or last, leader or follower. In a circle everyone is equally important. Use this time in the circle to pray for peace in the group, community, or world and to praise God.

You can also use the *Circle of Peace* for large group discussions or for processing an activity as it is a safe space to share ideas and learning.

Peacemakers Journal

A Journal notebook is a good way to let your young Peacemakers express their thoughts, ideas and understanding gained from the activities. It can be a simple notebook, a folder of loose leaf pages or a binder. It is used to process information and learning. Suggestions for topics for journaling appear at the end of each chapter and can be used after the various activities in that chapter. Remember that a journal contains the child's most personal thoughts and should be respected and read only with the child's permission.

Peacemaker's Journal Covers

Materials: Folder, magazines, glue, scissors, markers, pencil for each child.
 Purpose: This project helps children gain insight into themselves, while sharing with others. It introduces the concept that individual differences add interest to our world.

Ask the children to design covers for their journal folders using the materials available. Covers should describe their positive qualities and abilities. They might also include such things as their favorite color, book, movie, place, person, food, etc. and things about their family, ethnic background, skills, talents and hobbies.

When completed allow the children time to share their covers with one another.

Process the activity by discussing the following questions:
• If you made this cover two years ago how would it be different?
• If you made this cover two years from now how do you think it would be different?
• What did you discover about yourself? The members of your group?
• How do individual differences enrich our lives?

CHAPTER 1 Self-Image

When we know who we are, life takes on a new meaning. When we know what we are about, we are able to make better choices. What makes us unique is how we each relate to God, how we receive God's love, and how we choose to bring God's love into the world.

This chapter is about helping children develop a positive self-image by becoming aware of their relationship with God and the world. In this way they will be better able to make valuable contributions to the world around them.

We focus on two themes: I am a child of God, I am loved by God and I am made to bring love into the world. I am a Peacemaker who prays, studies God's Word, and works with others to solve problems.

Child of God

Music walk   10 minutes

Materials: Tape/CD player, tape/CD of lively music.

Purpose: These are "icebreaker" activities to help children relax with one another. They provide opportunities to introduce themselves, to show some creativity and to have fun.

A. Walk Ask children to walk around the room while the music plays. Tell them that you will call out a number when the music stops. They are to form groups of that many people. Ask them to introduce themselves and tell one interesting fact about themselves before the music starts again. Remind them to look for new people each time. Do this activity several times calling out small numbers (under five) and allowing time for children to complete the activity before restarting the music.

B. Space Ask children to walk around the room while the music plays. Tell them that you will call out a number when the music stops. They are to form groups of that many people. Call out large numbers (over five). When the groups are formed, ask them to occupy the smallest space that they can. Then ask them to occupy the biggest space that they can with each member touching at least two people. Do this several times.

C. Imagination Ask everyone, when the music starts, to walk around the room like a waiter. After a short time stop the music. Now ask them to walk around the room like a small baby. Continue the game suggesting they walk as if the floor was made of hot coals, as if the room was spinning and as if they were on the moon. Finally stop the music and ask them to walk as a very important person. Stop the music and point out that they are all Very Important People!

Create a Mini World

Materials: Clay or playdough, construction paper, tape, scissors, other creative materials.

Purpose: As children deliberate about creating their own world they will come closer to realizing that there is a purpose for our real world and for their place in it.

Group the children into pairs or trios. Invite them to take a few minutes to imagine a new world. Ask the following questions:

•What would life be like in your ideal world?

•Who would live in it?

•What would they need?

•What things would happen there?

•How would they happen?

•What does the world need to thrive?

•What would destroy it?

Allow the children to select materials to create a mini world based on their ideas. As they work they think up a story to share about this world. Allow as much time as possible for this project. Several hours over several days would be ideal. If time is limited you might use only markers and paper to create a world. When the project is complete give each group a chance to talk about their worlds and share their stories.

Process the activity by discussing the following questions:

•What is your hope for your world?

•As your world's creator what would you be willing to do to support your world?

•What do you think is the hope of the Creator for our world?

•What do you think our Creator is willing to do to support us?

Peace is not simply the absence of war . . . .
Peace is the active presence of Justice. It is Shalom, the well-being of all.

—*Rev. Allan Boesak*

Creation Story

20–40 minutes

Materials: Bible, story, or video about the Creation.

Purpose: This is a logical follow-up to *Create a Mini World*, though it can be used on its own. The purpose is to help the children personalize the creation story, finding themselves as important characters in God's ongoing story.

Tell the story of God's creation as found in Genesis, Chapters 1 and 2. Discuss the following questions:

- What are some of the things that God created?
- Why did God create them?
- Who are the inhabitants of God's world?
- How do they live?
- What does the world need to thrive?
- What would destroy it?
- What do you think is God's hope for the world?
- What do you do to bring this hope alive?

Puzzling It Over

15 minutes

Materials: 20–30 piece puzzle.

Purpose: To help the children realize the unique contribution each person makes to God's creation.

Briefly tell about God's creation pointing out that the world and we in it are created in love and need to live interdependently in order to survive.

Divide puzzle pieces among the children. Allow time for them to assemble the puzzle. Ask the children to complete the metaphor: We are each like a piece in God's big puzzle because _____ .

Some Ideas:

- Though we fit together to make a whole, we are each uniquely made, no two pieces are alike.
- Sometimes we have to turn ourselves around or upside-down in order to fit properly.
- No one else can fill our space. If we are not allowed to fill our space it will remain empty.
- If we refuse to fit then we will be alone outside the picture and the puzzle will be incomplete.

Peacemakers

Prayer   15 minutes

Materials: Copies of the *Prayer Of Saint Francis* (p. 1).

 Purpose: Children learn that prayer must be the basis for all action.
          They are introduced to the *Prayer of Saint Francis.*

Peacemaking must be grounded in prayer. Ask the children if it is possible for one human being to bring total peace to the world. Whose help do we need? (*Each other and God*) How does God know we need help? (*We ask.*) What do we call it when we ask God for help? (*Prayer*)

Suggest that the group ask God today to bless our world with peace. Share with them the *Prayer of Saint Francis.* Talk about the meaning of the prayer and its challenge to us. Set a prayerful mood and recite the prayer together.

Write a Prayer   30 minutes

Materials: Paper and pens.

 Purpose: This activity extends the concept that prayer is the core of Peacemaking.
          It offers an opportunity to cooperate with a group.

Group the children into pairs or trios. Suggest that they ask God today to bless our world with peace. Ask them to name areas in the world where peace is lacking. Have each group compose a prayer of five or six sentences.

Suggest that in the prayer they:
• Address God in whatever way they choose.
• Tell God what the problem is that they see.
• Ask God to help them in some specific way.
• Thank and Praise God.

They can be general, praying for all poor people or all children who live in violence. They can be very specific, praying for one person that they saw today. Their prayer can be conversational or poetic or any style they choose. Tell them that the prayer will be read aloud later. Allow the groups to go off to a quiet space and talk a bit before they actually write the prayer.

Read over each prayer as it is completed. Tell the groups to practice reading it aloud. Instruct them to copy the prayer in their journals. Conclude by having them bring their journals to the *Circle of Peace* to read each prayer.

Wildlife Rescue

Materials: Masking tape. For each group: one coffee can filled with rocks and a large #64 rubber band. For each person a 2½' length of rope or string.

Purpose: Solving this puzzle requires group communication and cooperation.

Preparation: Using the masking tape mark off a circle, about 5' in diameter on the floor for each group. Place one coffee can of rocks in the center of each circle.

Form groups of about six. Give each group the strings and a rubber band. Ask them to imagine that they are a wildlife research group studying in a remote area. They have found a nest of eggs on a small grassy area surrounded by quicksand. The nest seems to have been abandoned. Their task is to move the nest of eggs (coffee can of rocks) from the center of the quicksand to the outside of the circle using all and only the materials given. NO PART OF THE BODY IS TO ENTER THE CIRCLE OR EXTEND OVER THE TAPE! The entire group must be involved in the completion of the task. Be patient. Let them figure out how it can be done.

Process the activity with the following questions:
- How long did it take to figure out a solution?
- Did you have more than one solution?
- If so, how did you decide which solution to use?
- Did everyone seem to cooperate?
- Who would you say was the leader of your group?
- Would it have been possible for one person to get the eggs?
- Is it possible for one person to bring total peace to the world?
- Whose help do we need?

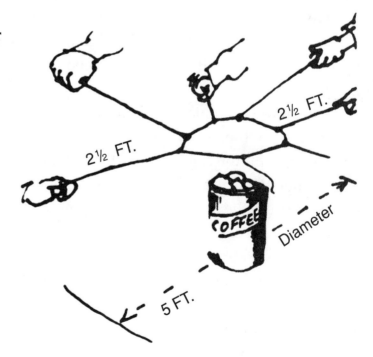

Find the Scrolls
45 minutes plus 1 hour preparation

Materials: *Gospel Teachings Sheets* (p. 9), 8 small color-coded containers for each group (film canisters, plastic eggs, small bags, etc.), Bibles or New Testaments, tape, colored paper.

Purpose: This very active game requires teamwork as the children become aware of Jesus' teachings about being Peacemakers.

Preparation: Before the activity prepare containers for the search.

Prepare for the activity

Make copies of the *Gospel Teachings Sheets*. Be sure there is a different Gospel passage for each small group.

Assign each passage a different color. Then, cut apart the individual verses of each scripture passage. Be sure to keep the Scripture reference attached to the first verse. Roll the verses into "scrolls."

Place the scrolls into the matching color-coded containers. Be sure there are eight containers for each group. Finally, hide containers throughout the designated area.

Form small groups of children. Explain how the Gospels hold a treasure of information on how to live as Peacemakers but that we need to seek to find it.

Show a sample container and assign a color to each group. Set the boundaries for searching and explain that the group needs to work together. Send the groups to find their eight containers.

When all the containers are found, the children read their scrolls and put the scripture together. Use the Bibles to find the scripture reference and put the verses in order. Tape the verses in order on the colored paper. Read the entire passage a few times.

Assemble the *Circle of Peace*. Have someone from each group read their Gospel teaching. Process the activity by discussing the following questions:
- Just as Jesus came to teach us how to live as Peacemakers, what is the message of your passage about being a Peacemaker?
- Do you think the message is easy to follow?
- How does your passage relate to your own life?
- What does it mean to be salt or light?
- Do you really think you can love your enemy?
- In the reading from Luke, what does John say to bullies?
- How is it that when you do something for others you are also doing it for God?

GOSPEL TEACHINGS

Matthew 25:34–40

The king will say to those on his right, 'Come, you who are blessed by my Father.

Inherit the kingdom prepared for you . . .

For I was hungry and you gave me food, I was thirsty and you gave me drink,

a stranger and you welcomed me, naked and you clothed me,

ill and you cared for me, in prison and you visited me.'

Then the righteous will answer him and say, 'Lord, when did we see you hungry . . .

or thirsty . . . a stranger . . . or naked . . . ill or in prison . . . ?'

And the king will say to them . . . 'whatever you did for one of these least . . . , you did for me.'

Matthew 5:43–45

You have heard that it is said,

'You shall love your neighbor

and hate your enemy.'

But I say to you,

love your enemies, and pray for those who persecute you,

That you may be children of your heavenly Father,

for he makes his sun rise on the bad and the good,

and causes rain to fall on the just and the unjust.

Luke 3:10–14

The crowds asked him, 'What then should we do?'

He said . . . , 'Whoever has two cloaks should share with the person who has none. And whoever has food should do likewise.'

Even tax collectors came . . . and said . . . , 'Teacher, what should we do?'

He answered . . . , 'Stop collecting more than what is prescribed.'

Soldiers also asked him, 'And what is it that we should do?'

He told them, 'Do not practice extortion.

do not falsely accuse anyone.

and be satisfied with your wages.'

Matthew 5:13–16

You are the salt of the earth.

But if salt loses its taste, with what can it be seasoned?

It is no longer good for anything but to be thrown out . . .

You are the light of the world. A city set on a mountain cannot be hidden.

Nor do they light a lamp and then put it under a bushel basket;

it is set on a lampstand, where it gives light to all in the house.

Just so, your light must shine before others, that they may see your good deeds

and glorify your heavenly Father.

Balloon Harvest

Materials: Blown up balloons of three different colors (lots of them).

Purpose: In a society where competition is the norm, children need to learn that in some cases, when the goal would benefit the common good, **cooperation** is superior to **competition.** We purposely allow the children to misinterpret the directions, making their discovery more profound.

Ask the children to form two groups. Line up sitting on the floor, one child behind the other, leaving space at the front and back of the lines. Name each group after one of the balloon colors (ex., red, blue). Explain that the goal of this activity is to move the balloons from the front to the back of the room as quickly as possible using only hands.

Several leaders (*may be children*) stand at the front of the lines and begin throwing balloons of all three colors at both lines. Another leader (*adult*) times the activity and observes the action. Frequently children assume that this is a competition between the two colors and behave accordingly.

After they finish, gather the balloons at the back and count them. Report on the time it took. Then, make observations around the following questions:

- How many balloons made it to the back?
- How many balloons of each color made it to the back?
- Were there any balloons that did not make it to the back? What color were they? Were they the color that matched the groups' names?
- Which balloons did the members of each line hit most often?
- Was the task accomplished?

Remind them that the task was to move the balloons from the front to the back of the room as quickly as possible using only hands. Repeat the activity. Time and observe. Repeat until the children understand that both groups have to work together to accomplish the task.

Process the activity by discussing the following questions:

- What did it take for us to complete this task?
- Did you think this was a competition when we started? Why?
- What makes you think that groups have to compete?
- Is it possible for one human being to bring total peace to the world?
- Whose help do we need?

Light of Peace

Materials: Baby food jar and votive candle for each child, colored tissue
paper, white glue or ModPoge®, scissors, markers, waxed paper.

Purpose: This craft project emphasizes the importance of prayer to peacemaking.

Preparation: Cover work space with old newspaper and gather all materials.

Instruct children to cut tissue paper into small pieces about one-inch square. They are to glue the squares to the outside of the jars overlapping the edges. Cover the bottom, sides and top edges of the jars. Write name or initials on one square before it is glued on to help identify the child's jar. Turn the jar upside down on a sheet of waxed paper. Cover with a thin layer of ModPoge® or glue. When dry, remove from the waxed paper and place the votive candle inside.

Bring the candles to the *Circle of Peace* for prayer.

Journaling

Materials: *Peacemaker's Journal* and pens.

Purpose: Quiet journaling time helps each child reflect on the personal meaning
of each lesson.

During your time with the children encourage them to reflect and journal on any of the following ideas:

- Write a poem titled *I Know I Am Loved*.
- Draw a picture to answer: 1) *How do I fit in God's world?* and 2) *What qualities do I have that can help make the world a loving place?*
- If Jesus came to your home for a week what do you think He would say to you about how you use the gifts He has given you?
- Illustrate yourself as a young Peacemaker doing something at this time in your life and as a future Peacemaker doing something when you are an adult.
- Complete and explain these sentences: 1) *The hardest part of being a Peacemaker might be . . . .* and, 2) *The best part of being a Peacemaker might be . . . .*

STEPPING OUT AS A PEACEMAKER

Discuss the specific needs of the people in your community. Consider the gifts the young Peacemakers can bring. Plan an activity that will make a difference to a person or group of people in your community.

- Involve other adult volunteers in helping with a scavenger hunt to collect food and household supplies for a local food pantry.
- Volunteer to help clean the food pantry one day.
- Plan entertainment and refreshments for a party at an adult care facility.
- Paint wooden toys or collect children's books for a homeless shelter.

CHAPTER 2 Respecting Dignity

Dignity is a characteristic of all human beings and all living things. It comes from God who lives in us and brings us to life. It cannot be lost or stolen because God cannot be lost or stolen. It can, however, be forgotten or ignored.

When we forget that God lives in us and others we disconnect from our dignity and we think that we have lost it. The role of a Peacemaker is to remember God who lives in us and to help others to remember as well.

The purpose of this chapter is to help children become aware of God's presence in each human being. We encourage children to treasure their dignity and to respect the dignity of others. We focus on three themes: I am a unique and special child with dignity, I am called to recognize the dignity of others, and I am a Peacemaker who works to protect the dignity of others.

The coupon below will be used with the activity on page 18, "Finding the Gift."

Gift Coupon

I am a Child of God. I have dignity.
God made me out of love to bring love into the world.

ONE OF MY SPECIAL GIFTS IS:

_____

name _____

Child with Dignity

Hand Prints

40 minutes plus time for plaster to dry

Materials: 9" foil pie plates (1 per child), sand, Plaster of Paris®, water, markers, paperclips (1 per child), old newspapers.

Purpose: To recognize that one's dignity comes from God's love and is affirmed by others.

Have the children prepare the work area by covering it with old newspaper. Give each child a pie plate half full of damp sand. The children press one hand into the sand to make a hand print. Fill the pie plate with Plaster of Paris® mixed to directions. Show the children how to unfold the paper clip, then stick it halfway into the Plaster of Paris®, two inches from the edge. Let pie plates sit undisturbed until the plaster hardens.

When the plaster hardens the children can remove the cast from the sand, brush off the excess sand and print their name in the palm.

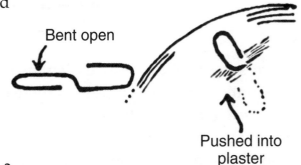

Bent open

Pushed into plaster

Read *Isaiah 49:15–16*. Talk about what it means. Ask the following questions:

- What kind of love never forgets?
- How does it feel to know your name is written on the palm of God's hand?
- What does this tell you about your dignity?

Sometimes it is hard to remember God's love for us. God gives us loving people who help us and protect us. They are living symbols of God's presence.

Encourage the children to name five people God has placed in their lives who remind them of God's love, who help them when things get difficult? (Be specific about naming five people who will really be of help. Ask how the person can help. It is important that children know there are people who are there for them.) Write the names of these people on the fingers of the hand casting.

Alternate Activity Use heavy paper and paint to make a hand print. Follow the same discussion process.

Right Before Your Eyes

45 minutes

Materials: For each child; 7" X 2½" block of wood, 1/4" square furring strips cut into the following lengths: six 2", two 1½", two 7/8" and six 5/8", black paint, paint brushes, wood glue, rulers.

Purpose: To create an optical illusion where the name of Jesus is present but not always visible to everyone.

Paint the blocks of wood with black paint. Allow time to dry. Carefully place furring strips in the pattern shown at right. Then, glue strips in place.

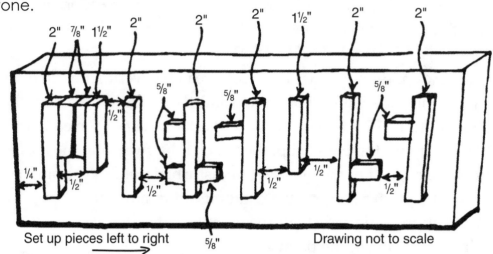

Set up pieces left to right ⟶   5/8"   Drawing not to scale

Process the activity by discussing the following questions:
• Even though the word **Jesus** is there on the plaque not everyone can see it. Once you see it, can you still lose sight of it?
• If you do lose sight of it can you still believe the word **Jesus** is there?
• God lives in each person. Can we lose sight of God in us? Can we lose sight of God in another? Losing sight of God doesn't mean God is gone. How do Peacemakers treat themselves and others even when it is hard to see God in them?

Going On a Trip

15 Minutes

Materials: *Characteristics* poster (p. 15).

Purpose: To help each child identify their unique characteristics.

Allow time for the children to reflect on their most positive qualities. Give some examples from the *Characteristics* poster as suggestions.

An adult begins the game by saying, "I am _____. I'm going on a trip and I am bringing my _____ (*Naming her unique characteristic*)."

Go around the room with each child completing the same sentence and adding the name and characteristic of each previous player. Example: "I am David. I'm going on a trip and I am bringing my good sense of humor, Molly's courage and Jim's honesty . . . . " The adult ends the game by repeating all previous responses. It is okay if characteristics are repeated.

CHARACTERISTICS

FAITHFUL	**COURAGEOUS**
LOVING	**JUST**
JOYFUL	**PATIENT**
KIND	**HONEST**
TRUSTWORTHY	**GOOD HUMORED**
OPTIMISTIC	**PEACEFUL**
GENEROUS	**THOUGHTFUL**
HARD WORKER	**EXCITING**

Recognizing the Dignity of Others

The Class Trip

Materials: Suitcase, stapler, *Characteristics* poster (p. 15), 3" X 5" index cards.
(Print one child's name on each card. Make 3 sets of cards.)

Purpose: To practice verbalizing positive observations about others.
To increase self-esteem by hearing positive comments from peers.

Give each child three index cards, each with a different child's name on it. Be sure no child gets their own name.

Provide time for the children to think about their friends whose names are on the cards. On each card they should write one positive characteristic appropriate to that child. They may use items from the list or some of their own.

When all are ready the children take turns walking to the suitcase and saying, "I'm going on a trip and I'm bringing Jose's kindness, Sophia's faithfulness and Rodney's good sportsmanship." The three cards are dropped in the suitcase. When all have finished affirming their friends in this way the cards can be taken out and handed to the children whose names are on them. Pass the stapler to attach the cards to their journals.

Process the activity by discussing the following questions:

• Was it difficult to think of positive words to write? Explain.

• How did it feel to hear positive comments about yourself?

• How does knowing people think these things about you affect your sense of dignity?

One must not love oneself so much as to avoid getting involved in the risks of life that history demands of us.... Let us all do what we can.

—*Oscar Romero*

Fill the Gap

Materials: None.

 Purpose: To experience that each person is valuable and needed.

Invite the children to stand in a circle with you. Step back out of your space. Note the gap in the circle. Direct the person to the left of the space to call out someone's name. The person called runs to fill up the space. The person to the left of the new gap should immediately call out another name to fill the new gap. Continue as quickly as possible.

Let confusion reign. End the game by asking everyone to go back to their original place. HA!

Basic Needs

Materials: 3" x 5" index cards (10 per child), pencils, masking tape,
        Category Cards.

 Purpose: To reflect on the essential needs of life.

Preparation: Make the Category Cards by writing one category word on each of nine 3" x 5" index cards—Food, Shelter, Clothing, Health Care, Education, Employment, Safe Environment, Love.

Ask children to think of what they absolutely need to live in our culture. Give them two minutes to write one thing on each card. Then, post the *Category Cards* on the wall.

Working together, sort everyone's needs into the categories by taping the cards under the appropriate heading. At this point try not to eliminate anything listed by the children, even if it seems frivolous or a tease. (For example, "chocolate" would go under **Food**, and "computer games" or "tickets to a basketball game" would go under **Health Care** because we need recreation to be healthy.)

Discuss the difference between **Need** (*something necessary for life*) and **Want** (*something desirable to make life more pleasant*).

Ask if the lists can be narrowed down to basic needs by eliminating wants. Invite the children to take down any cards they think are **Wants**. There may be some argument about whether or not something is a **Need**. In the end, if the children insist something is a **Need** leave it on the list. Later they may revise it on their own.

Sum up the activity by pointing out that people have a better chance of remembering their dignity when their basic needs are met.

Peacemakers

Finding The Gift

30 Minutes

Materials: Bibles, Gift Coupons (p. 12), small containers (plastic egg, film canister, small bag), small candies and pencils.

Purpose: To reflect on the possibility of helping another person regain a sense of dignity.

Remind the children that we all have dignity because we are children of God. We can never lose our dignity because God is always present in us. Sometimes life, itself, becomes a distraction and we forget our dignity or we forget about the dignity of others. Our job as Peacemakers is to love our neighbors and help them remember their dignity.

Read the story of *The Good Samaritan* (Luke 10:25-37). In the story of *The Good Samaritan* the stranger in the road had apparently lost his dignity.

Consider the following questions:

- How did each character treat him?
- How did the Samaritan's actions restore the stranger's sense of dignity?

Introduce the game by passing out copies of the *Gift Coupon*, pencils and containers. Invite the children to take a moment of silence to think of the gifts they have which would bring love into the world. If necessary offer a few suggestions. Instruct the children to fill out the coupons, fold them and place them in the containers. Collect the containers.

Move the children on to another activity while you or an aide secretly fill all the containers with candy and hide them. Make the hiding places challenging to find.

Later, setting boundaries, tell the children to find one container, not necessarily their own, and bring it back to the *Circle of Peace*. Each child should then take a turn carefully opening the container and reading the coupon. The author should step forth and the two children share the candies.

Process the activity by discussing the following questions:

- What could make a person forget about the dignity of another person?
- What could make a person forget about his own dignity?
- What are the ways we restore a sense of dignity? (*Hint: love, sharing our gifts*)
- How do you feel when you help restore someone's sense of dignity?

Peace Mural   30 minutes

Materials: A large sheet of butcher paper, masking tape, magazines,
glue, scissors, markers.

Purpose: To apply Pope Paul VI's quote, "If you want Peace, work for Justice"
to life today.

Introduce the quote "If you want Peace, work for Justice." Discuss what Pope Paul VI
means by this. What is Peace? What is Justice? How does one lead to the other?

Tape the butcher paper to a wall. Ask the children to search through the magazines to
find words or pictures to illustrate the quote. Make a collage by gluing these cut-outs to the
butcher paper. Allow time to admire and discuss the mural.

Gospel Dignity   30 minutes

Materials: Bible.

Purpose: To be aware of Jesus' call to care for one another.
To practice working together toward a common goal.

Read *Matthew 25: 31–40*. Discuss how Jesus calls us to respect each other's dignity by
caring for one another's needs. Name the specific actions Jesus prescribes. These are called
"Works of Mercy."

Form groups of three or four children assigning a number to each group. Explain that
you will read the passage again. This time, however, you will stop after a work of mercy
has been named. You will call out a number and that group is to portray the action by
forming a tableau. They will have only ten seconds to get into formation before you call
FREEZE. For example the first action is, "I was hungry and you gave me food." Group 1 is
to quickly portray this and stand still when you say, **FREEZE**.

Once you are certain the children understand the task proceed with the reading. Stop
after each work of mercy, call a group number and say, **GO**. Count to ten and say, **FREEZE**.
Allow the other groups time to admire the tableau. Read the next action and continue the
process through the end of the reading.

Process the activity by discussing the following questions:
• How did you like portraying these actions from the scripture? Was it hard
  or easy to work so quickly with your group? Why?
• How can helping others enable them to recognize their dignity? Could it ever
  make them feel less dignified? How?
• How can helping another make you more aware of your own dignity?

Journaling

Materials: *Peacemaker's Journal* and pens.

Purpose: Quiet journaling time helps each child reflect on the personal meaning of each lesson.

During your time with the children encourage them to reflect and journal on any of the following ideas:

- Think of a time when you were able to overcome a difficult challenge. Where was God in that time?
- The greeting, "God be with you," and the response, "And also with you," are salutes to one another's dignity. How is this true?
- Write about a person you know who lives with dignity in spite of their difficulties.
- The Catholic Church lists seven *Corporal Works of Mercy*: feed the hungry, give drink to the thirsty, clothe the naked, shelter the homeless, care for the sick, visit the imprisoned, and bury the dead. Write about someone you know who does these works. What are some ways that you can do these works?

STEPPING OUT AS A PEACEMAKER

Use *Matthew 25:30–41* as your guide to plan an action.

- Organize a clothing drive for needy children in your area. Collect only jeans and sweatshirts. Sort through to dispose of anything inappropriate. Pack the rest and deliver.
- Join a local ecology group to advocate care for a river, lake or ocean nearby.
- Order kits to make rubber welcome mats for an organization which provides housing for the poor.

While you are proclaiming peace with your lips,
be careful to have it even more fully in your heart.

—*Saint Francis of Assisi*

CHAPTER 3 Learning Compassion

Compassion is a deep awareness of the suffering of another and the desire to change it. We believe that children are naturally compassionate people who need adult encouragement to act on their feelings.

A compassionate person is an astute observer and attentive listener, one who takes personal interest in the well-being of others. Scripture often describes Jesus as being "deeply moved in spirit." So, too, a Peacemaker is moved to take action to relieve the suffering and restore dignity to every person.

This chapter is about recognizing the pain many people feel because of the injustice in the world. We will help the children understand the subtle ways in which people hurt one another. Finally the children may discern some simple steps toward lessening the suffering in the world. We focus on three themes: 1) I have compassion for those who suffer, 2) I live in an imperfect world, and 3) I can make a difference.

The Virtue of Compassion

Copycat
10 minutes

Materials: None.
 Purpose: To practice being observant of others.

Tell the children that compassion is a fundamental virtue in peacemaking. It is a deep awareness of the suffering of another and the desire to change it. Point out that to be compassionate requires skill in reaching out and observing others.

Form groups of 6–8 children. Ask each group to sit in a circle. Each child will perform a simple action, like a wave of the hand. The child on the left must repeat this action and add a new one. The activity continues around the circle at least twice, each child repeating all the previous actions and adding a new one. When the small groups have been successful, combine the groups and try it again as one big group.

Process the activity by discussing the following questions:
- How did you know what to do when it was your turn? Explain.
- What was the difference for you in the small group and in the large group?
- What does this game have to do with compassion?

Bible Puppets/Pantomime

1 hour

Materials: Bibles, clean old white socks, markers.

Purpose: To examine Jesus' teaching on compassion.

Choose a Bible passage you wish to use from those listed (or use one of your favorites that is concerned with compassion). Form small groups according to the passage chosen.

Give each child a sock and some markers. Designate the character each child will portray during the reading. Ask the children to make the sock into a puppet for this character by drawing faces with the markers. After five or ten minutes put markers away and settle the children for the reading. As you or the narrator read the passage the children are to use their puppets to act out and/or say the lines of the passage. Read slowly. Repeat if necessary. Don't have time for puppets? Do it as a pantomime only.

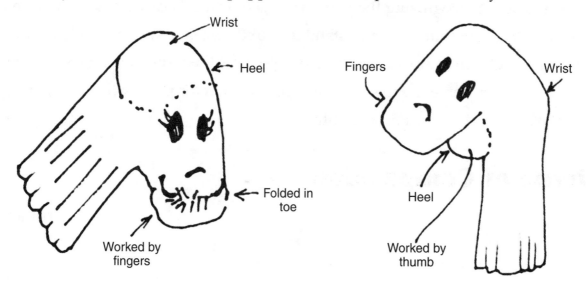

Scripture Readings: Matthew 25:31-46, Luke 3:10-14, Mark 10:46-52, Mark 10:13-16
John 13:4-14, Luke 16:19-26, Luke 10:25-37, Luke 17:11-16

Process the activity by discussing the following questions:
- Jesus gives the same message over and over. What is He telling us about the poor and downtrodden?
- What does He tell us about being rich or powerful?
- Do you think Jesus loves poor people more than He loves the rich? Explain your answer.
- What was Jesus' point in washing the feet of the apostles?
- Make a list of the responsibilities people have toward one another.
- We say Jesus had compassion for the poor and downtrodden. How would you define compassion?

Saint Thérèse Beads

Materials: 12" length of dental floss or lanyard, 10 pony beads,
a small plastic cross charm, scissors for each child.

 Purpose: To provide a tool for remembering acts of compassion.

Saint Thérèse, known as the "Little Flower," dedicated herself to a lifestyle she called "The Little Way." She tried to do all things, no matter how small, as best she could to honor Jesus. She lived in service of others, giving them her best attention and care. To do this she had to be aware of each person's needs. She had to be compassionate.

Pass out the materials. Fold the lanyard in half in order to find the center. String the cross on the lanyard and hold it at the center spot with a knot.

String the ten beads, one at a time as shown in the diagram. Insert one end of the lanyard through the hole of the bead. Then insert the other end of the lanyard through the same hole from the opposite direction. Slip the bead down toward the cross. Add the next bead in the same way inserting one end of the lanyard through the hole and the other end through the same hole from the opposite direction. Repeat until all beads are assembled, leaving a small space between each bead. Tie a knot at the top and trim off any excess lanyard.

Show the children how the beads can be slipped towards the cross, one at a time, each time they perform an act of compassion. Challenge them to move all ten beads before your next meeting.

*Be sure to point out kind acts when you observe them
to remind the children to move their beads.*

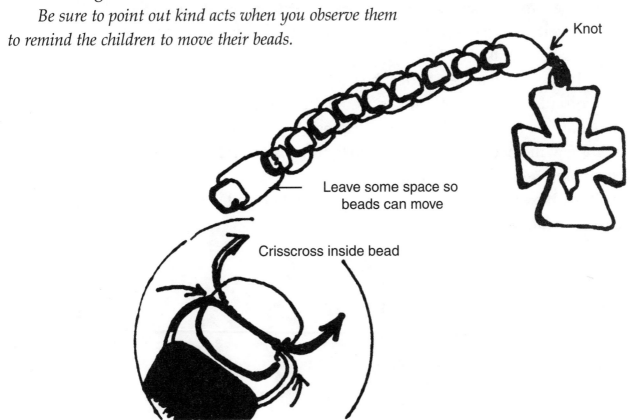

Knot

Leave some space so
beads can move

Crisscross inside bead

Imperfect World

Wall of Prejudice

45 minutes

Materials: Boxes (empty milk cartons or shoe boxes) one for each child,
permanent markers, paper to wrap around the milk cartons, tape.

Purpose: To examine the consequences of prejudice.

Remind the children that prejudice is a judgement made about a person or thing without full knowledge or examination of the facts. Ask for some examples such as, "I hate people who smell bad", or "I only like people who wear clothes from The Gap®."

Form two groups. Give each child a box and a marker. Instruct the children to compose a typical remark spoken in prejudice as follows: 1) one group should complete the sentence, *I don't like people who . . .* and 2) a second group should complete the sentence, *I only like people who . . . .*

Have the children write the sentences on their boxes. Both groups bring their boxes to a designated line, one group sitting on each side of the line. Taking turns they read their sentences and place their boxes on the line, building a wall.

With the children still sitting on each side of the wall discuss the following questions:
- If you really believed what you wrote, would it be easy to be friends with this wall between you?
- Which is the stronger barrier, the boxes or the attitudes written on them?
- What would it take to remove the barrier? (*Change in attitude*)
- What can a Peacemaker do? (*Educate*)

Give the children time to reconsider the prejudiced statements they wrote on the boxes. Ask them to formulate a more informed statement to replace the one they put on the box. For example, *I like the person but hate her smell.* And, *It doesn't matter where people buy their clothes.* After a few moments invite them to take turns coming to the wall, making their new statement and removing their box.

When all the boxes have been removed, cross the line and offer a sign of peace. If possible share a treat together.

Pig Latin

1 hour

Materials: Pencils, Ulturalcay Ingobay sheet (p. 28) for each child.

Purpose: To experience the difficulty of being in an unfamiliar situation.

Ask how many children have ever moved from one country to another, one town to another or transferred from one school to another. What was it like for them? Did they feel any prejudice in these situations?

Continue the discussion in this direction: 1) One common prejudice is to look down on people who don't speak our language clearly, 2) What are some things people say when they meet people who cannot speak English well?

Ask the children to imagine being with a group of kids who speak a language you don't understand, in a school with books you can't read and adults giving directions you can't comprehend!

Explain that in this activity they will experience what that might feel like by using a language some might be familiar with: Pig Latin.

How to Do It!

SPEAK PIG LATIN

- If a word begins in a consonant, take the first letter or pair of letters, move it to the end of the word and add **ay**.

  Examples: Pig = ig + pay = **igpay**   Latin = atin + lay = **atinlay**

  blend = end + blay = **endblay**   think = ink + thay = **inkthay**

- If a word begins with a vowel, say the word and add **yay**.

  Examples: animal = animal + yay = **animalyay**

  understand = understand + yay = **understandyay**

- If a word is one letter, such as "a" or "I", say the word and add **yay**.

  Examples: a = **ayay**   I = **Iyay**

Practice these phrases with the children:

- My name is _____ .   Ymay amenay isyay _____.
- I would like to eat now.   Iyay ouldway ikelay otay eatyay ownay.
- Where is the bathroom?   Erewhay isyay ethay athroombay?

Explain to the children that from the time you say, **Ogay!** until they hear a hand clap like this (demonstrate how you will clap your hands), there will be no English allowed in the room. Only Pig Latin may be spoken. In the meantime the group will play a game. Ask if there are any questions. When all understand the process, begin the game.

Say: **Ready, Set, Ogay!**

Pass out the **Ulturecay Ingobay** sheets and give these directions:

Ethay amegay eway illway ebay ayingplay isyay alledcay **Ulturecay Ingobay.** Aketay ethay eetshay aroundyay ethay oomray andyay askyay ouryay iendsfray otay ignsay ayay aresquay atthay asksyay ayay estionquay ichwhay eythay ancay answeryay. Orfay exampleyay, ifyay ouryay iendfray ancay ingsay ayay ongsay inyay anotheryay anguagelay, ehay oryay eshay ouldshay ignsay atthay aresquay

Enwhay ouyay avehay ourfay aressquay inyay ayay owray, eitheryay erticallyvay, orizontallyhay oryay iagonallyday, ouyay allcay outyay **Ingobay!** Enwhay eway avehay reethay **Ingobays**, eway illway ignalsay ethay endyay ofyay ethay exerciseyay. Etgay Ityay? Oday ouyay avehay anyyay estionquays? Eginbay!

English Translation ————————————————————————

The game we will be playing is called **Cultural Bingo**. Take the sheet around the room and ask your friends to sign a square that asks a question which they can answer. For example, if your friend can sing a song in another language, he or she should sign that square. When you have four squares in a row, either vertically, horizontally or diagonally, you call out, **Bingo!** When we have three **Bingos**, we will signal the end of the exercise. Get It? Do you have any questions? Begin!

When three bingos are called end the exercise. End the use of Pig Latin by clapping the signal and revert back to speaking English.

For a more complete experience you may want to extend the use of Pig Latin to include another activity like a craft or snack time. (It is important that the children have adequate time to experience the difficulty of being in an unfamiliar situation.)

Process the activity by discussing the following questions:

- Which was easier: speaking, listening to or reading Pig Latin? Explain.
- How did you know how to play the game? Did you understand the spoken directions? Did you deduce the procedure from looking at the sheet? Did you observe others playing the game and copy their actions?
- If you didn't understand what someone was saying, what clues did you use to translate the message?
- How did you feel when you were playing the game?
- How did you feel when the game was over? What would it be like if the game never ended and you had to work in a foreign language all day every day?
- Today we were all in the same boat, trying to work with a different language. Some of us were more familiar with it than others. Some picked it up much more quickly than others. How did it feel if you were slower in catching on to it? Would it feel different if only you were unfamiliar with the language and everyone else was comfortable? How would it feel?
- Having played this game, do you think you will be more compassionate to people who are just learning our language? Does the game remind you to feel compassion for anyone else?

To show great love for God and our neighbor, we need not do great things. It is how much love we put in the doing that makes our offering something beautiful for God.

—*Mother Teresa of Calcutta*

ULTRALCAY INGOBAY

Ancay ouyay amenay wotay itiescay inyay Russia? 1	Atwhay isyay insideyay ayay Piñata? 5	Avehay ouyay everyay ademay ayay Hajj? 9	Oday ouyay acticepray Tae Kwon Do? 13
Amenay wotay ountriescay inyay South America. 2	Oday ouyay owknay anybodyyay owhay entway otay Africa? 6	Owhay asway Ghandi? 10	Atwhay isyay Kwanza? 14
Atwhay isyay elebratedcay onyay Cinco de Mayo? 3	Ancay ouyay eatyay ithway opstickschay? 7	Avehay ouyay everyay eatenyay aviarcay? 11	Ancay ouyay aysay "eacepay" inyay ivefay anguageslay? 15
Avehay ouyay isitedvay eethray ountriescay? 4	Atwhay isyay ayay ainstickray? 8	Ancay ouyay ingsay ayay ongsay inyay anotheryay anguagelay? 12	Amenay eethray Ativenay Americanyay ibestray oryay ationsnay. 16

ULTRALCAY INGOBAY
Answer Key

1. Can you name two cities in Russia?
   Moscow, Saint Petersburg, Novgorod, Irkutsk and others

2. Name two countries in South America.
   Argentina, Bolivia, Brazil, Chile, Colombia, Ecuador, Paraguay, Perú, Uruguay, Venezuela and others

3. What is celebrated on Cinco de Mayo?
   Mexican Independence, May 5, 1862

4. Have you visited three countries?

5. What is inside a piñata?
   Candy and small toys (a papier mâché or clay figure hit with a stick, by a blindfolded child, to get the goodies)

6. Do you know anybody who went to Africa?

7. Can you eat with chopsticks?

8. What is a rainstick?
   An African rhythm instrument

9. Have you ever made a Hajj?
   A pilgrimage to Mecca

10. Who was Ghandi?
    An Indian leader and teacher of nonviolence

11. Have you ever eaten caviar?
    Eggs of a large fish

12. Can you sing a song in another language?

13. Do you practice Tae Kwon Do?

14. What is Kwanza?
    African American celebration of unity

15. Can you say "Peace" in five languages?
    Shalom (Hebrew), Mir (Russian), Pax (Latin), Paix (French), Paz (Spanish)

16. Name three Native American tribes or nations.
    Algonquin, Apache, Cherokee, Cheyenne, Iroquois, Mohawk, Navajo, Seminole, Sioux, and others

I Can Make a Difference

Hoop Dream

10–20 minutes

Materials: Two or three Hula Hoops®.
Purpose: To build teamwork.

Ask the children to stand together in a circle and join hands. Explain that they are to pass a Hula Hoop® around the group without it touching the floor and without breaking the chain of hands.

Place the hoop in the circle so that two players have their hands locked together through the hoop. At your signal they are to start passing the hoop around. Applaud everyone when they finish. Try it several times.

Make it tougher by adding a second hula-hoop and require that one go clockwise and the other counterclockwise around the circle. Try other variations.

Process the activity by discussing the following questions:
- What made the activity easy to accomplish?
- What made it tough?
- What did you learn?
- What did you have to be willing to do?

A Compassion Story

20 minutes plus 26 minutes for the video

Materials: *Horton Hears a Who* Video (MGM, United Artists Home Video, 1970), TV/VCR.
Purpose: To exemplify compassion in action.

Introduce Dr. Suess' character, Horton, the elephant, as a good example of a compassionate spirit. He firmly believes that, "A person is a person no matter how small." He is willing to risk a lot in order to help the "little Whos of Whoville." Show the video.

Process the activity by discussing the following questions:
- In what ways was Horton willing to sacrifice for the little Whos?
- What adjectives would you use to describe Horton's character?
- What attitudes threatened to destroy the Whos?
- Are there real people today who might be in trouble like the Whos?
  Discuss them and their difficulties. What might help them?
- Was there ever a time when you felt like Horton?

Raindrops 20 minutes

Materials: Script for *Raindrops* (p. 32), *Charity and Justice* poster (p. 33).
 Purpose: To introduce the concepts of Charity and Justice.

Ask for 8-10 volunteers to prepare a skit. Give them the script and bring them to a separate space to practice. One person will narrate. The others will pantomime. Encourage exaggerated actions and facial expressions. Allowing less than ten minutes to assign parts and practice will make the skit more spontaneous and, therefore, more fun.

Assemble the rest of the group as an audience and introduce the skit.

After the skit is performed, process the activity by discussing the following questions:

• What was the first thing that had to be done when the water came in?

• Was that enough to solve the problem?

• Was it a good idea to look outside? Why?

• Why didn't some children care about finding the source?

Explain that Peacemakers are committed to helping people in need. There are two general ways people help out. Show the *Charity and Justice* poster.

The first way deals with the immediate needs such as grabbing buckets and mops. It is called **Charity**. The second way goes to the root of the problem to make changes necessary to reduce the occurance of need such as going outside. It is called **Justice**.

Peacemakers are called to perform works of **Charity** or **Justice** or both. Mother Teresa did **Charity**, Martin Luther King did **Justice**, Dorothy Day did both.

Peace is a daily, a weekly, a monthly process, gradually changing opinions, slowly eroding old barriers, quietly building new structures. And however undramatic the pursuit of peace, that pursuit must go on.

—*John F. Kennedy*

Raindrops Script

Narrator reads the script. (Be aware of the pronoun choices at various spots in the narrative.*)

The Peacemakers were bored.

Sitting in their clubhouse, they wondered what they could do.

They muttered, "What can we do? I'm bored. What, oh what, can we do?"

Suddenly a drop of water fell on one child's head. Then another. And another.

Quickly someone jumped up and grabbed a bucket to catch the drops.

Someone grabbed a dishpan.

More water came in.

Someone grabbed a pot. Someone grabbed a cup.

More water came in.

The peacemakers were determined to save the floor.

"Save the floor! Save the floor!" they shouted.

More water came in.

Some grabbed mops. Some grabbed rags, to wipe up the floor.

They were working hard, running to and fro with containers catching the drops.

One looked out the window.

* "Hey, it's not raining out!" he/she called.

"So what?" asked the others.

* "Where is the water coming from?' he/she asked.

"Who cares?" replied the others. "At least we're not bored anymore."

* "I'm going to check it out." he/she said, running out the door.

* Outside he/she found a group of kids with a hose squirting the roof of the clubhouse.

"Hey," the Peacemaker called. "What are you doing?"

The kids dropped the hose and ran away.

Inside the clubhouse the water stopped coming in.

The Peacemakers finished cleaning up. They hung the towels out to dry. They put away the mops and buckets and other containers. Then they sat back down.

(*Pause*)

"I'm bored." said one Peacemaker. "What can we do?" said another.

CHARITY AND JUSTICE
TWO TYPES OF ACTION FOR PEACEMAKERS

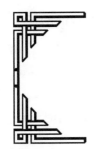
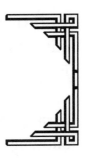

CHARITY

1. Response to accidental events such as fire or flood and to critical situations such as homelessness or hunger.

2. Spontaneous. Help goes directly to victims. No concern about causes.

3. Temporary. To satisfy immediate needs.

4. Non-controversial actions.

JUSTICE

1. Response to human systems or institutions such as racism or unjust laws.

2. Planned and organized.

3. Provides for permanent change at the root of the problem.

4. Controversial actions, not always easily accepted by society.

Journaling

Materials: *Peacemaker's Journal* and pens.

Purpose: Quiet journaling time helps each child reflect on the personal meaning of each lesson.

During your time with the children encourage them to reflect and journal on any of the following ideas.

- Name a character from a movie or TV program who shows compassion for the poor or downtrodden. Briefly describe what he or she does. How does this person remind you of yourself?
- Choose one of the following problems: homelessness, hunger, unemployment, lack of health care, or poor air and water. Name some solutions. Classify the solutions as either **Charity** or **Justice**.
- Design a poster telling people what you learned about prejudice.
- Illustrate how prejudice interferes with compassion.

STEPPING OUT AS A PEACEMAKER

Choose a need in your community or in the world at large. Make a difference by using *Charity and Justice* as your guidelines.

- List the needs of your local community as seen in recent news stories. Decide how you can address a need. Do it!
- Choose a need from your list and find out what is being done to change the situation. How can you help?
- Write to local officials and churches asking their help in changing the situation.
- Focus on a country that has been in recent news stories. Decide what the country needs to improve its situation. How can you help? Do something!
- Launch a campaign to collect medical supplies, blankets or money to send to a country in need.
- Write letters to the editors of local newspapers and national magazines to educate the public on the needs of one country.
- If appropriate, write letters to congressmen, the President of the United States or other public officials with suggestions for our foreign policy.

CHAPTER 4 Exploring Forgiveness

Forgiveness is letting go of resentment and agreeing to love unconditionally. It is one of the most difficult teachings of Christ. There is no peace without forgiveness.

In this chapter the children will study the Biblical teachings about forgiveness. They will look at the world to see where forgiveness is needed. We will challenge the children to be "Ambassadors of Reconciliation." We focus on three themes: As a child of God I am called to forgive others, I know that forgiveness is absolutely necessary for a peaceful world, the Peacemaker in me can forgive others.

Called to Forgive

Reverberations

10 minutes

Materials: None.

Purpose: To illustrate the lasting effects of violent actions.

Adult leader stands in the center of the *Circle of Peace* and demonstrates two hand signals. Hands held straight up over the head indicates **Make noise**. Hands held down at the sides indicates **Silence**. Instruct the children to watch the leader carefully. When hands are up they should make as much noise as possible: screaming and yelling, stomping feet, clapping hands, whatever they can do without leaving their place. When hands are dropped all noise is to stop instantly. Children should then close their eyes and listen waiting until the reverberations from the noise are totally still within them. When they are at peace, they can open their eyes and look at the leader.

Leader signals to begin the noise. Time it for about thirty seconds. Signal for silence. Time the silence until all eyes are looking at you. Compare the times of "violence" (*noise*) and "recovery" (*silence*).

Process the activity by discussing or doing the following:
- Compare the times.
- Share feelings.
- Pray.
- Sit quietly.

Dots to Wisdom

Materials: Copies of *Dot Problems* (p. 37), pencils, Bibles.

Purpose: To practice creative problem solving. To consider forgiveness as an alternative to revenge.

Pass out the *Dot Problems*. Read the directions. Instruct the children to work by themselves or with a partner to come up with solutions. Do not solve the problem for them. Do not even give them hints. Allow enough time for the children to either solve the problems or give up.

Share solutions. Ask the children what made the problem so difficult. The expectation is to stay within certain parameters. The solutions lie outside those parameters. It takes a creative mind and a courageous spirit to move beyond the normal way of doing things and find a better way.

Tell this story:

When a young teacher was shot to death by students in Arkansas, her husband was filled with rage and despair. He hated the boys who carried the guns, he hated their parents and grandparents, he hated society in general for depriving him of the woman he loved more than anyone and for taking a mother away from their son. For months he struggled with caring for his son while searching for retribution.

Ask: • What would be the expected way for the father to act toward the students?
        • Do you think he could ever forgive them?

Continue the story:

After months of struggling the father finally realized that he could not raise his son to be a man of peace if he did not have peace in his own heart. So he began to work on forgiveness. The result was not only beneficial to the students facing criminal charges, it was also beneficial to the young father and his son. They have put the rage behind them and are moving forward towards a full life.

Ask: • Is this response out of the ordinary?
        • How does forgiveness help the criminals? The father? His son?

Pass out Bibles:

Read *2 Corinthians 5:17–20* and *Matthew 6:9–15*. Point out that Peacemakers are **Ambassadors of Reconciliation**. They pray with Saint Francis, "Where there is injury let me sow pardon." They pray with Jesus, "Forgive us our trespasses as we forgive those who trespass against us." Refusing to forgive escalates the problem.

Ask: • Do you think there can be peace without forgiveness? Explain.
        • Where do we get the power to forgive?

DOT PROBLEMS

1. Make a square larger than
   the original square by
   moving only two dots.

2. Use four straight lines to connect
   all the dots below. You may not lift
   your pencil while drawing the lines
   or go back over any of the lines.
   You can only cross each dot once.

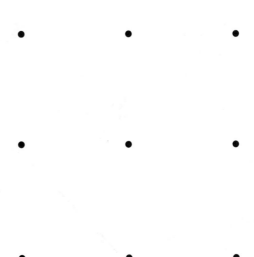

DOT PROBLEMS Solutions

1. Make a square larger than
   the original square by
   moving only two dots.

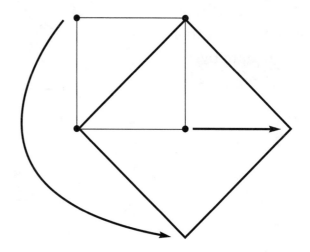

2. Use four straight lines to connect
   all the dots below. You may not lift
   your pencil while drawing the lines
   or go back over any of the lines.
   You can only cross each dot once.

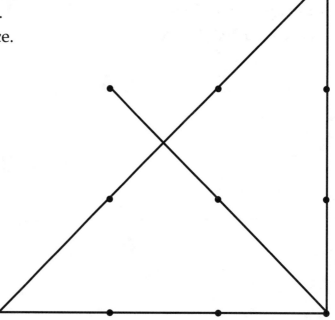

Forgiveness Is Necessary

Letting Go
30–60 minutes

Materials: 1 hand-sized rock per child, table or altar with a crucifix, reflective music, player, copies of the *Prayer of Saint Francis* (p. 1)

Purpose: To reflect on the burden of resentment.

As the children enter the room hand each a small rock. Tell them that they are to hold on to their rocks until given permission to put them down. They may move the rock from one hand to another, but they may not, under any circumstances, put the rock down.

Proceed with a normal session letting the children maneuver around the rocks in their hands. Assign a journaling page, do a simple craft like designing a felt banner or play a game. Have no mercy about holding the rocks. After 20 or 30 minutes call the children to the *Circle of Peace*.

Process the activity by discussing the following questions:
- How are you feeling about the rocks in your hands?
- How did holding the rock affect your work today?
- Would you like to set it down? Not Yet!
- Imagine that the rock is a bad feeling you have about someone who has hurt you in the past. Imagine that the only way that you can let go of this feeling of resentment is to forgive the person. Can you do it? What happens if you can't?

Begin the reflective music. Say in a calm voice, "Take a few minutes now to be quiet." After a period of quiet time give the following directions pausing between each.
- Think about whether or not you are holding on to a real resentment.
- Has it been getting in the way of your being a Peacemaker?
- If you can forgive the person bring the rock to the cross and give it to Jesus.
- If you can't forgive yet bring the rock anyway and ask Jesus to help you move closer to forgiveness.
- If you carry no resentments it is definitely time to put the rock down.
- Use no words. Move when you are ready.

Let the music continue to play.
Say no more until all the rocks have been laid down.
Pray the *Prayer of Saint Francis*.

Newspaper Wall   10 minutes (ongoing)

Materials: Bulletin Board, mural or newsprint, newspaper and
           magazine articles, staples or glue, scissors.

 Purpose: To highlight worldwide situations where forgiveness is lacking.

Designate and prepare a bulletin board, mural or poster to display the cut out articles.
Bring in one or two articles that show a lack of forgiveness in the world. Invite the children
to bring in others as they find them. Explain that as children bring in articles the group will
read them and try to understand the situations. The articles will then be added to the
display to remind us of the need to forgive.

Process the activity as new clippings are added by discussing the following questions:
• What is the situation?
• Do we have all the information we need to understand it?
• What needs to be forgiven?
• What is keeping the people involved from forgiving each other?

Extension: Ask the children to begin looking for articles or stories in their lives that tell
what happens when people forgive. Add them to the wall and highlight in some way what
happens when people forgive.

> **W**hy, then, should we act in the peace movement?
> So we can discover the source of violence in our
> own hearts.
>
> **—Henri Nouwen**

Forgiving

From Tears to Peace
30 minutes

Materials: For each child, worksheet *From Tears to Peace* (p. 42), markers or crayons, scissors, glue, red construction paper, tape or CD player, and meditative music.

Purpose: To explore the idea that without forgiveness there can be no peace. If appropriate, to celebrate the Sacrament of Reconciliation.

Discuss these two aspects of forgiveness: 1) We must forgive those who have hurt us, and 2) We must ask forgiveness of those we have hurt.

Point out that without forgiveness there can be no real peace. Ask the children for examples of this. Begin playing music softly. Invite the children to quiet themselves and think about how much God loves them. Pass out the worksheets and crayons or markers.

In a quiet voice instruct the children to color in the teardrops using one color for the empty spaces, another color for the spaces with one dot and a third color for the spaces with two dots. Make corrections as you see fit.

As they color, ask the children to think about someone who has hurt them. Encourage them to ask God to help them forgive that person. They should also think about someone whom they have hurt. Invite them to tell God how sorry they are and ask for forgiveness. Be silent with only the music playing until all have finished coloring the teardrops.

Pass out the scissors, glue and red construction paper. Show the children how to cut out the teardrops and, matching the dark circles, glue them onto the paper. Turn the paper around making a heart with the word, **Peace**.

If you are able and it is appropriate, have a priest available for the Sacrament of Reconciliation. Invite the children to bring their hearts to the confession room to ask God's forgiveness and to pray for the grace to forgive the people who have hurt them.

Close with an *The Lord's Prayer*. There is no need to process this activity.

From Tears to Peace

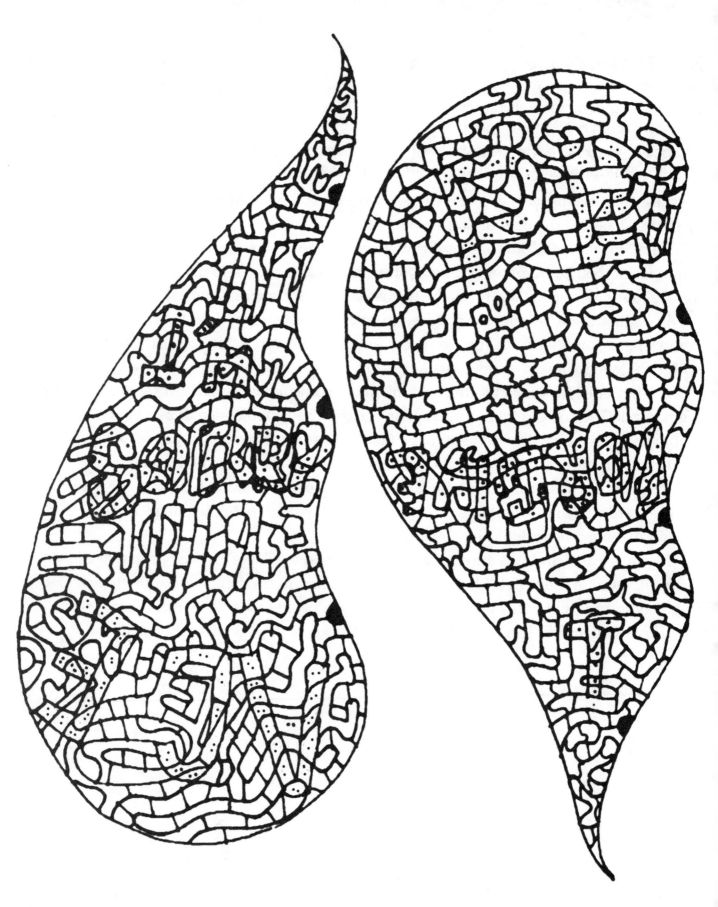

Journaling

Materials: *Peacemaker's Journal* and pens.

Purpose: Quiet journaling time helps each child reflect on the personal meaning of each lesson.

During your time with the children encourage them to reflect and journal on any of the following ideas.

- The effects of violence take a while to stop, even after the violence stops. Explain.
- Why can "Ambassadors of Reconciliation" also be called "Peacemakers?"
- What can I do when I just can't forgive?
- Write a prayer for a country torn apart by resentment.

STEPPING OUT AS A PEACEMAKER

Choose an appropriate day (World Peace Day, Memorial Day, etc.) around which to organize a prayer vigil. Invite all the people in the community to attend.

Design a prayer for reconciliation between people of different countries, different ethnicities, different genders or different sexual orientations to be used at the prayer vigil.

CHAPTER **5** Effective Communication

Effective Communication is essential to any peacemaking effort. So often conflicts arise out of misperceptions and/or unclear expectations. To work together we need to understand each other clearly. When we give children the skills both to express their needs and desires and to listen with respect, we open the door to opportunity.

The goals of this chapter are to help children express themselves clearly and confidently and to practice active listening.

Water Balloons   30 minutes

Materials: Balloons filled with water, at least one per pair of children, *Sender/Receiver* poster (p. 45).

Purpose: To demonstrate the concepts of *sender* and *receiver* in effective communication.

Instruct the children to choose a partner and form two lines facing one another with partners directly across from each other. The lines should be about three feet apart. One partner holds the water balloon. At the signal the balloon is carefully tossed to the other partner. If the balloon is caught without bursting, the partners each take a step back and toss again. When the balloon bursts, the partners step out of line and sit on the sidelines until the game ends. The play continues until all but one pair are still standing with their balloon intact.

Process the activity by discussing the following questions:

• We will call the person throwing the balloon the **sender** and the person catching the balloon the **receiver**. What did the sender have to do to keep the balloon from bursting? (*Possible response: Look at the receiver, aim, throw with the right amount of force.*) What did the receiver have to do? (*Possible response: Watch the sender, be willing to move to catch the balloon, catch it before it hit the ground.*)

• Would you throw if the receiver wasn't looking at you? Would you turn your back if the balloon was coming toward you? What did you try to do when the balloon went way to the right or the left? What would happen if you just stood in one spot?

Display the *Sender/Receiver* poster. Explain that playing with the water balloons is much like communicating. There is a **sender** who speaks and a **receiver** who listens. Can you think of other ways the game is like verbal communication?

(*Possible response: The sender and receiver are frequently reversing roles. Each must pay attention to the other by watching and listening. Each must be willing to do what it takes to make it work.*)

If time permits play another round.

Sender/Receiver

Sender:
Look at the receiver,
aim, throw with the right
amount of force.

Receiver:
Watch the sender,
be ready to move if needed,
catch the balloon before it lands.

Listen and Watch

Materials: For Game 1, two drawing pads and markers.
For Game 2, 3" x 5" index cards, timer.

Purpose: To demonstrate the importance of listening and observation in effective communication.

GAME 1

Arrange the children in a circle. Ask for two volunteers who like to draw pictures. Invite them to sit in the middle of the circle, backs to each other. Give each a drawing pad and marker. Tell one child that you will write a word at the top if his paper which he is not to reveal to the other volunteer. He is to draw a picture of that word. As he does so, he is to tell the other volunteer how to draw the same picture. The other child is to listen to the instructions and follow them as best she can. When they are finished, they can compare pictures to see how closely they resemble one another. Play three or four rounds.

Ask:

• Receiver, would it have been easier to do if you could have used your eyes to see what the other was talking about?

• Sender, would it have been easier to give directions if you could see how the other was interpreting your words?

GAME 2

Preparation: On each 3" x 5" index cars, write the title of a song, movie or book. You may also use a simple common phrase such as "He who hesitates is lost."

Ask for a new volunteer who likes to act. Using the instructions on page 47, explain how to play *Charades*. The volunteer picks a phrase, silently reads it and takes thirty seconds to gather her thoughts. She then pantomimes for all the other children. The timer is set for three minutes. The children call out ideas until the complete phrase is identified.

The round ends when the phrase is guessed correctly or when the time is up, whichever comes first. If the group fails to guess, the volunteer reveals the answer. Play three or four rounds.

How to Do It!

PLAY CHARADES

Charades is a game in which words or phrases are represented in **pantomime**, sometimes word-by-word or even syllable-by-syllable, until they are guessed by the other players. There are some universal signs for playing this game:

- Begin by holding up fingers to indicate the number of words in the phrase. Then hold up fingers to indicate which word in the phrase is being pantomimed.

- Pull one ear to indicate "sounds like" if you pantomime a word that rhymes with the word being guessed.

- If the word needs to be divided into syllables, hold up fingers to indicate the total number of syllables in the word, then tap those fingers on your arm. Hold up the number of the syllable being pantomimed.

- When the word is guessed point to your nose and begin the next word!

And we are put on earth a little space,

That we may learn to bear the beams of love.

—*William Blake*

Do What It Takes

Materials: A blindfold; *Effective Communication* poster (p. 49); hoops, balance beam, traffic cones, hurdles and/or other objects to make an obstacle course. (Don't overlook natural obstacles like trees.)

Purpose: To understand the importance of personal effort in effective communication.

Preparation: Before the children arrive, build an obstacle course with at least five challenges. Keep it relatively easy as the child engaged in it will be blindfolded.

When the children arrive, have them form groups of three. Explain that one member of the group will be a **Guide** and one will be a **Coach**. They will be leading the third member, the **Challenger**, through an obstacle course. The Challenger will be blindfolded. After a minute to assign their roles, ask all Challengers to leave the room with an adult.

While the Challengers are gone walk one child through the obstacle course so the others know what is expected. Then send the child through again, timing the endeavor. Let that time plus 20 seconds be the norm for all other attempts.

The Guide will walk next to the blindfolded Challenger to make sure she doesn't stray too far or get into dangerous situations. For the most part, the Guide should not talk.

The Coach will sit at the end of the course. He will call out directions to the Challenger bringing her through the course.

Groups will go one at a time. An adult will time each effort. The goal is to get as close to the norm time as possible. One at a time, have the Guides bring their Challengers in, to take a turn at the course. The Challengers should not be allowed to watch another group until they themselves have completed the course. Tell the Challenger that the goal is to complete the course as close to the norm time as possible. In the end congratulate all the groups for a good effort.

Process the activity by discussing the following questions:

- Coaches, what were your difficulties in bringing your challenger through the course? Overall was it easy or hard?
- Guides, how did you feel walking beside the Challenger? Were you tempted to talk at all? Were you ever worried?
- Challengers, what was the hardest part of completing the course? Were the Coaches' directions clear enough? How did the Guides help you?
- Everyone, how effective was the communication between your group members? Do you think they all gave their best personal effort? What would have happened if someone didn't try?

Display the *Effective Communication* poster. Discuss each step in relation to the game you just played.

Effective Communication

1. **Know what you want to say.**

   Be clear in your mind of the message you plan to send.

2. **Know to whom you are speaking.**

   Be aware of the situation.
   Be aware of your relationship with the listener.

3. **Get the listener's attention.**

   Be sure the listener is hearing what you say.
   Use the listener's name.

4. **Use your senses to notice responses.**

   Be aware of the listener's reaction to your message.
   Be aware of the listener's feelings.
   Notice the listener's body language.

5. **Use understandable language.**

   Consider your message and the person to whom
   you are speaking.
   Be willing to choose new words and try a new way
   to send your message.

Change Partners

15 minutes

Materials: Pencil and paper.

Purpose: To experience the frustration of being interrupted.

Have the children choose partners and play the game, *Hangman*. Let them know that they should continue playing for the time allotted. Advise them that you will call out **Change Partners** after a short while. At that time the child guessing the word should get up and move to the next seat so that all have new partners. When a word is guessed the other child selects a new one and the game continues. Allow the children to start playing. After about one minute call, **Change Partners**. Give them time to get back into the game and call, **Change Partners** again. Do this several times. After about ten minutes call a halt to the game.

Process the activity by discussing the following questions:
• How did you feel during this game?
• How many words were guessed?
• What might have made it easier to play the game?

Relate this experience to the experience of being interrupted during a conversation. Is communication effective if it is constantly being interrupted by the listener?

The "I"s Have It

30 minutes

Materials: Several pairs of bar magnets, two stickers labeled *I* and *You*, *I Statements* poster (p. 52).

Purpose: To introduce the benefits of *I Statements*.

Invite the children to play with the magnets for a few minutes. Take one bar magnet and place the **You** sticker on one end and the **I** sticker on the other. Hold up the bar magnet with the word **You** so the children can read it. Move it toward a second bar magnet in such a way that it will be repelled (*to the like pole of the second magnet*). Tell the children that language can be like this. Sometimes we say things in such a way that we inadvertently push people away.

Turn the labeled magnet so that the opposite pole **I** will be attracted to the second magnet (*to the unlike pole of the second magnet*). Tell the children that Peacemakers need to find the words that bring people together.

Explain that in everyday life conflicts, problems or misunderstandings are bound to happen, even between friends and family members. The words we choose to address these issues can make a big difference in how they are resolved.

When we start a sentence with **You** such as **You always** or **You didn't**, we put the other person on the defense. He might feel blamed or put down before we even finish our sentence. (*Demonstrate again with the magnet.*)

Peacemakers: The New Generation

If, however, we start with **I** such as **I feel** or **I am**, we keep the responsibility for our feelings and that gives the other person a chance to listen better. (*Demonstrate again with the magnet.*)

Example:

You didn't invite me to your party!

The **You Statement** sends a strong message of blame.

How different it would feel if one heard,

I feel disappointed that I wasn't invited to your party.

The **I Statement** leaves room for discussion.

Display the *I Statements* poster. Walk the children through the steps. Offer a few examples of your own. Ask for volunteers to practice changing the following **You Statements** into **I Statements**. Be sure they follow the four steps on the *I Statements* poster. Allow the other children to help form statements if the volunteer is stumped. Be patient. This is not an easy concept to internalize.

```
YOU STATEMENTS

You shouldn't call me that name.
You make me so mad.
The next time we go shopping you should . . .
Don't you think that you should . . .
Why don't you just stop it!
```

Ask for volunteers to practice using **I Statements** in the following situations. Again, be prepared to offer help. Be insistent, however, on following the four prescribed steps.

1. A friend dares you to shoplift.
2. Someone in school calls you a bad ethnic name.
3. Your friend accuses you of talking behind her back.
4. A teacher accuses you of cheating.
5. A parent blames you for your brother's mess.
6. A schoolmate tells your friend that you are fat.

After all this practice, encourage the children to try this at home. Next session briefly discuss the results of their effort. Stories are usually interesting and positive.

Please note: Using **I Statements** *is a fundamentally important aspect of effective communication. It is also a difficult skill to develop. Be prepared to review this lesson several times.*

I Statements

1. SAY THE PERSON'S NAME

Joanne

2. SAY HOW YOU FEEL

I feel rejected.

3. TELL WHAT CAUSED YOUR FEELING

When you don't include me in deciding how I can help

4. ASK FOR WHAT YOU NEED

Please let me decide if I can do it.

What does it mean?

Materials: *Non-Verbal Message Cards. (See below.)*
 Purpose: To recognize non-verbal messages.
Preparation: Make the Non-Verbal Message Cards *by writing each one of the non-verbal messages from the list below on a 3" x 5" index card.*

Give each student one *Non-Verbal Message Card.* Explain that when you call a name, that child will stand and try to convey that message to the class without talking or making any sound. As soon as the group correctly guesses the meaning, the child will sit down and you will call the next person.

See how many the class can get in the time allotted. Give them about five minutes.

NON-VERBAL MESSAGES

Stop	Go	Yes	No	OK
I don't know	I'm busy	Hello	Good-bye	I'm interested
I'm bored	I don't care	I'm telling the truth	He's smart	Peace
Wrong answer	You did well	I love you	Great game	You are right
We won	Victory	He's crazy	Come here	Go away

Include any others you would like to add.

Process the activity by discussing the following questions:
•What was hard, what was easy about this activity?
•Why is it important to read non-verbal messages correctly?
•Why is it important to send the correct message with our body when we are talking with someone?

If you love peace,
then hate injustice, hate tyranny, hate greed—
but hate these things in yourself, not in another.

—Gandhi

Listening for feelings

Materials: *Feeling Statement Cards, Feeling Words* poster (p.55)

Purpose: To practice identifying the speaker's feelings.

Preparation: Make the *Feeling Statement Cards* by writing each one of the feeling statements from the list (below) on a 3" x 5" index card. Display the *Feeling Words* poster

Pass out one *Feeling Statement Card* to each child. Tell them that they will be asked to read the statement to the class using one of the feelings indicated on the card. The class will then identify the feeling expressed. Refer to the *Feeling Words* poster. Remind them that there may be more than one way to read the statement. Give them about thirty seconds to prepare, then begin. Call one child at a time. As soon as the group guesses the correct feeling move on to the next child. See how many they can identify in five to ten minutes.

If you have more time ask the children to read the statements again in a different way and have the class guess the new feeling expressed. *Adaptation:* Have the children write their own feeling statements.

Feeling Statements

- I just can't figure it out. I give up. (Angry / Disappointed)
- Wow! Eight days until Christmas vacation. (Excited / Overwhelmed)
- Look at the picture I drew! (Proud / Embarrassed)
- Will you be calling my parents? (Guilty / Confident)
- You never get mad at him, always me. (Resentful / Sad)
- I'm getting a new 10-speed bike. (Happy / Tense)
- Yeah, I guess I was mean to her. I shouldn't have done it. (Sorry / Guilty)
- Am I doing this report right? Do you think it will be good enough? (Insecure / Surprised)
- You Narc! You'd turn in your own brother. (Angry / Friendly)
- I can do this part on my own. I don't need your help. (Respectful / Elated)
- Leave me alone. Nobody cares what happens to me anyway. (Depressed / Humiliated)
- I'd like to tell him that, but I just can't. (Terrified / Tired)

Process the activity by discussing the following questions:

- How did you know the feeling? In communication non-verbal clues such as facial expression, words, tone of voice, and body language are often as important as the words used.
- Why is it important to listen for feeling when we communicate?
- Is it possible to misinterpret feelings in conversation? What can we do?

FEELING WORDS

Happy	Loving	Elated
Thrilled	Surprised	Excited
Confident	Friendly	Respectful
Affectionate	Proud	Sure
Disappointed	Angry	Jealous
Terrified	Guilty	Resentful
Humiliated	Tense	Miserable
Depressed	Tired	Lonely
Sorry	Sad	Insecure
Embarrassed		Overwhelmed

Time's Up

Materials: Candy bars or prizes, clock with a second hand, *Effective Listening* poster (p. 57).

Purpose: To practice effective listening.

Ask for a volunteer to play a game and possibly win a small prize. Tell the volunteer that you are going to tell him a story and he is to stop you by saying, **Time's Up** when exactly one minute has passed from the moment you say, **Go**. Tell him that if he is within three seconds of the goal he will win a prize. Tell him that you will ask questions along the way which you expect him to answer. Be sure he cannot see a clock or a watch. Appoint a time keeper to sit behind the volunteer and record the time elapsed. Remind the time keeper and the rest of the group that they may not signal the volunteer about the time.

Say, **Go**, and begin telling a familiar story, such as *Peter Pan* or *Cinderella*, stopping every few seconds to ask simple questions which demand his response (*Do you see what I mean? What was her name again?*). After about thirty seconds, turn and direct the rest of the group to move in some way (*stand up, form a circle*). Talk until the volunteer says, **Time's Up**. If he is within three seconds give him the prize. If there is time repeat with another volunteer.

After the game ask if it was difficult to listen to you. What might have gotten in the way of the volunteer's listening?

Remind the children that effective communication requires the best efforts of both the sender and the receiver. If you have previously examined the *Effective Communication* poster you may want to review that now.

Say, "The receiver, or the listener, has a particular role to play in making the communication work." Display the *Effective Listening* poster. Discuss each step.

If you have already done the activities, *What Does it Mean?*, *Listening for Feelings*, or *Change Partners* you may refer back to them as they relate to body language, listening for feelings and interrupting.

When the children seem confident with the concepts, form groups of three. Assign three roles: **Speaker, Listener, Observer**. Point out that the **Observer's** role is to watch and listen then report to the other two how well they conformed to the directions on the *Effective Listening* poster.

Give the **Speakers** the first assignment. Time them for two minutes. Signal, **Time's Up.** Give the **Observers** a chance to report on what they saw and heard.

Direct the groups to change roles. Repeat the activity using a new topic for discussion. Change roles one more time and repeat the activity. *Note: Be sure to insist on precise reports from the Observers. Ask questions such as: What did her body language tell you? How do you know she was watching for feelings?*

After the third practice round briefly summarize with the children what was learned.

Effective Listening

1. GIVE FULL ATTENTION

Show interest and acceptance
by your body language.
Avoid distractions.

2. TRY TO UNDERSTAND

Listen to words.
Watch for feelings.
Ask simple questions to clarify.

3. DO NOT INTERRUPT

Getting the Message

30 Minutes

Materials: *Role Play Scenario Cards.* (See below.)

Purpose: To practice effective communication skills.

Preparation: *Write each one of the role-play scenarios (see below) on a 3" x 5" index card.*

After reviewing the skills introduced in this chapter, ask for volunteers to act out several role plays. Divide the *Role Play Scenario* cards between them. Assign the other group members the task of observing the communication between actors.

- Some Observers will evaluate how the message was sent. Did the Speaker have the Listener's attention? Did she use clear language? Did she use non-verbal clues? Were **I Statements** used well?
- The other Observers will watch for listening skills. How did the Listener show attention? Did he interrupt the Speaker? Did he listen for feelings as well as words?

Introduce the first *Role Play Scenario.* Afterward allow the Observers to tell what they witnessed. Continue until time runs out.

Role Play Scenarios

- One classmate accuses another of gossiping about her.
- Someone describes his success in the day's basketball game.
- A mother and son disagree about the clothes he wants to wear to school.
- A father teaches his daughter how to bait a hook for fishing.
- Two friends argue about inviting a new kid to go bowling with them.
- One friend gives another directions to her home.

Journaling

15 minutes

Materials: *Peacemaker's Journal* and pens.

Purpose: Quiet journaling time helps each child reflect on the personal meaning of each lesson.

During your time with the children encourage them to reflect and journal on any of the following ideas.

- Think of your favorite TV show. Describe the communication between the characters. Is it effective or not?
- What are some things you can do to make communication more effective in situations when some people can't see, hear or speak?
- Some people enjoy playing charades, others have a hard time with it. How did you feel? Explain.
- It isn't always easy to recognize non-verbal messages. Tell a story of a time when things got all confused because of a misunderstanding of them.
- Tell about what happened when you used "I" statements with a family member or a friend.

CHAPTER 6 Anger Management

Anger is an extreme reaction to a situation or event. On the positive side it acts as a signal that something important to one's life is being threatened. It has an energizing effect, mobilizing the body for self-defense and providing the stamina to complete difficult tasks. On the other hand, anger can interfere with one's rational thought patterns, causing impulsive behavior. It can evoke aggression. Anger is a problem when it is too common or too intense, lasts too long or disrupts relationships.

The goals of this chapter are to help children understand the positive and negative aspects of anger, to reflect on the cause of their own anger and how they respond to it and to search for creative ways to handle it.

That Burns Me Up! 30 Minutes

Materials: Drawing paper, pencils, markers, masking tape.
 Purpose: To reflect on causes of personal anger.

Distribute paper, pencils and markers. Instruct the children to draw a cartoon of something that really makes them angry. When all are completed, invite each child to stand up, display his cartoon by taping it to the wall and complete this sentence, "When _____ , that burns me up because _____ !"

After everyone has taken a turn, process the activity with the following questions:

- Look at all the cartoons. Is there anything there that doesn't really make you angry? What does this tell us about anger? (*Anger is a personal feeling.*)
- There is a wide variety of reasons people get angry, some much more serious than others. Can you see a common thread in all the cases we've talked about? What is one thing that is true of each case? (*The cause of anger directly disturbs the peace of the angered person.*)
- If anger is caused by a disturbance to our peace, what should be our goal in handling our anger? (*To restore peace.*)

Peace is not merely the absence of war . . . Instead, it is rightly and appropriately called an enterprise of justice.

—*The Church in the Modern World, number 78*

Is It Really Me?

Materials: Masking tape, *Six Styles of Anger* cards and *Six Styles of Anger* poster. (p. 61 and p. 62).

Purpose: To introduce different styles of handling anger.

Preparation: 1) Make cards by copying the Six Styles of Anger worksheets (1 and 2) for each group of three to five children. Cut the pages on the heavy lines to make cards with one symbol or written description on each. 2) Enlarge one copy of each of the 6 symbols on the Styles of Anger 2 worksheet. Post these at eye level around the room.

Form groups of three to five children. Distribute one set of symbols and anger style descriptions to each group. Allow five to ten minutes to read the six descriptions of anger styles and match them with a symbol. *(Explosive Anger/Firecracker, Stony Anger/Rock, Boiling anger/Teakettle, Spicy Anger/Hot Pepper, Oppressive Anger/Dump Truck, Controlled Anger/River)*

When the task is completed, direct the children to choose the style that best describes how they handle anger, find the appropriate symbol on the wall and stand near it. Allow time for them to read and find their spot. Allow talking and encourage cooperation. Help anyone who cannot decide between one symbol or the other. Explain that most people have a mixture of styles. They should pick the one that seems the strongest in them.

When all have found their places ask them to share with the other children at the same location to discover similarities and differences among them. Ask them to choose a spokesperson to share their understanding of this style with the rest of the class. If someone is alone at a symbol go and discuss with her.

Give each group a few minutes to share their observations. After each sharing summarize the presentations and remind the children that there are positive and negative aspects with each style. Try to discover some of the positive aspects for each style.

Process the activity by discussing the following questions:
- How easy was it to choose your personal style of handling anger?
- Did everyone in your group react exactly the same way? Explain.
- Do some styles seem more productive than others? If so, in what way?
- Were you able to find positive aspects for each style?
- Is it helpful to understand your anger style? Explain.

Instead of loving what you think is peace, love other men and women and love God above all else.

—*Thomas Merton*

SIX STYLES OF ANGER 1

Explosive Anger I've got a pretty short fuse. The smallest thing can set off an explosion of rude words and gestures. I'm almost always angry with someone about something. Even if things seem fine to everyone else, I'll find an excuse to be angry.	**Spicy Anger** My anger is hot and quick. I let people know directly and truthfully how I'm feeling. Then I can let go of the issue and be friends again. I'm not always tactful. Sometimes I hurt people's feelings without meaning to.
Stoney Anger I don't like to admit it when I'm angry. I try not to show any emotion. If someone offends me, I'll keep it to myself and walk away. Sometimes I go weeks without speaking to a person. My silence is the punishment for them.	**Oppressive Anger** I often dump my anger on someone weaker than me, even if she/he had nothing to do with the offense. I tend to overreact, being more angry than the situation would cause. I tend to blame my troubles on others.
Boiling Anger I keep my anger inside until it escapes in steamy sarcasm or teasing. Sometimes I don't even know I'm feeling angry until someone asks what is my problem. Keeping it all in can make me tired and even sick.	**Controlled Anger** I work hard to keep my anger from running out of bounds. I take time to cool down and understand my feelings. I think of ways to solve the problem without attacking the other person. I talk it out and let it go.

SIX STYLES OF ANGER   2

Good News/Bad News

45 Minutes plus 85 minutes for video

Materials: *Anger: Good News and Bad* poster (p. 64), newsprint and
marker, video, *Running Free*, from Columbia Tri-Star, TV/VCR.

Purpose: To demonstrate the positive and negative aspects of anger.

Open the discussion with a statement in this vein: "The lunchroom is closed because of remodeling. The good news is we can eat lunch outside picnic-style. The bad news is we can't get to the lemonade." Talk about how often in life one thing can have two aspects, positive and negative. Give an example like snow on Christmas Eve. Ask for volunteers to name a good thing about that and a bad thing about it.

Label two columns on the newsprint: **Good News** and **Bad News**. Give the children the following examples and ask them to write items under each title for them:

•The eye doctor prescribes glasses for you.

•The principal declares a snow day.

•The TV breaks down.

•The ball game is rained out.

•There are eight people for dinner and six slices of pie.

•You have outgrown your favorite sweater.

•The family can't afford a vacation this year.

•You are angry because the new kid in class is being teased.

Ask the children how anger can be both good new and bad news. Have them explain their answers. Display the poster, *Anger: Good News and Bad*. Discuss the positive and negative aspects of anger.

Introduce the video, *Running Free*. Tell the children to watch for displays of anger in this movie. How do the characters use their anger? Is it good news or bad? Show the video.

Process the activity by discussing the following questions:

•Anger which is motivated by compassion and love is **Just Anger**. It can lead to actions which bring peace to the world. Anger which is motivated by prejudice or hatred is **Unjust Anger**. It can lead to pain and suffering. What examples of anger did you see in *Running Free*? Would you say they were **just** or **unjust**? What were the results of the angry feelings?

•Lucky was justly angry at Caesar for preventing the freedom of the other horses. How did he handle his anger? What was the result? What do you think might have happened if he had used his strength to kill Caesar?

•Saint Augustine said, "Hope has two beautiful sisters, anger and courage." What do you think this means? Do you think he was referring to **Just Anger, Unjust Anger** or any anger? Can you give an example from *Running Free*?

•Is there anything in today's world that causes you to feel **Just Anger**? What can you do to change it? Do you need to be older? Do you need help? Who can help you?

ANGER: GOOD NEWS AND BAD

HERE'S THE GOOD NEWS

Anger helps us know that something is wrong.

Anger prepares our bodies for self-defense.

Anger can motivate us to make a difference.

Anger gives us energy to act.

Anger gives us fortitude so we can follow through
on difficult challenges.

Anger can help us be good Peacemakers.

HERE'S THE BAD NEWS

Anger can muddle our thinking
and confuse the issues.

Anger can hide our true feelings of fear

or sadness or disappointment.

Anger can cause us to act inappropriately.

Anger might last so long or be so intense that
it interferes with our relationships.

Anger can result in violence.

Anger can prevent us from being good
Peacemakers.

Instruments of Peace

Materials: A wide variety of art supplies: paint, clay, sponges, pipe cleaners, fabric, etc., *Steps to Peacemaking* poster (p. 66), cards with *Role Play Scenarios* printed on them. (See below.)

Purpose: To consider how anger can be used for positive purposes.

Preparation: Copy one role-play scenario on each of five 3" x 5" index cards.

Invite the children to choose a partner. Engage them in a project to make an interesting gift/card for a specific event in the near future. (Holiday, Get Well, etc.) Tell them to work as a group using any of the materials provided.

After about 30 minutes ask the groups to share their products with the whole group. Take time to compliment their creativity.

Say, "You were very clever about how you used the instruments and materials provided to make someone happy. A Peacemaker's job is to bring love into the world. Would it surprise you to learn that anger can also be an instrument for peace? It is, if you know how to use it."

Display the *Steps to Peacemaking* poster. When we're feeling anger, we have two choices. We can use our anger to take steps to hurt or to make peace. Review the *Steps to Peacemaking* poster. Ask for volunteers to role play some situations where anger can be used to create something positive. *Note: It may be necessary to walk the actors through two or three situations one step at a time to help them practice the sequence.*

Role Play Scenarios

- A new student from another country comes to your school. She sits at your table at lunch. Some of your tablemates tell her to go away. "We don't eat with foreigners," they say.
- The school bully takes your only pen just before a big test. You ask him to give it back. He responds, "Come and get it, Wimp."
- You miss an important play in the last soccer game. The coach yells at you in front of the team and fans.
- You have been teamed up with another student to do a project for English. You will share the final grade. You have worked hard on the project. Your partner has blown it off. You'd like an A, but fear the final project will earn a C.
- You and your sister, Carrie, are getting ready for school when you notice that she is wearing your shirt which you just washed. Carrie took the shirt without asking.

Process each role-play as it is completed using the poster.

STEPS TO PEACEMAKING

1. CALM DOWN
Pull back a bit from the situation.
Name your feeling and what is causing it.
Do something to relax: breathe deeply, exercise,
listen to music, talk to a trusted friend.

2. BE DISCREET
Choose a time and place where
you can talk with no distractions.

3. SPEAK OPENLY
Be honest and respectful.
Use I Statements.

4. LISTEN CAREFULLY
Keep an open mind.
Be an effective listener.

5. REACH AGREEMENT
Be creative.
Stay focused on the problem.
Choose a solution which satisfies all persons involved.
Commit to a plan of action.

Journaling

Materials: *Peacemaker's Journal* and pens.

Purpose: Quiet journaling time helps each child reflect on the personal meaning of each lesson.

During your time with the children encourage them to reflect and journal on any of the following ideas:

- Write out an action plan for handling your anger in a positive way.
- Tell how you can use the positive aspects of anger to change a situation at school or home.
- Illustrate the following with words or pictures. "It makes me angry to think that some people live in hopelessness. It will take courage to make a difference for them. Here's an example."

STEPPING OUT AS A PEACEMAKER

Develop a process for dealing with anger in your group. Perhaps a designated space for talking it out, maybe a mediator to help things along. Would you put posters there? How would you decide when and by whom the space would be used?

CHAPTER 7 Conflict Resolution

Conflict occurs naturally in any relationship. Resolving conflict in a just and peaceful manner takes patience, persistence and desire. It also takes some skill. Knowing what to do in a critical moment can allay the temptation to hit and run.

The goals of this chapter are to help the children analyze conflict, to give them some steps they can take toward peaceful resolution and to give them opportunities to practice the techniques.

Friends and Enemies   45 Minutes

Materials: A 6' length of rope.

Purpose: To experience the difference between cooperation and competition. To consider how to face situations as friends rather than enemies.

Form two groups of children. Find a large enough space (maybe outdoors?). Play *Tug of War*. Play several times as time permits.

Sit on the ground and talk about the feelings experienced during the game. Help the children realize that there was always a winner and a loser and that each had different feelings.

Form groups of 6–10 children. Have the children stand close together. Take the rope and tie all the children in one group together. You may run the rope between them over and under the different children to make it more complicated but do not tie it tightly. Give them time to feel "tied up." Tell them they can now get out of the situation. Let them figure it out themselves. Offer encouragement. Other classmates can offer encouragement as well. Repeat until all the children have had a turn.

Sit down and talk about the experience. How did they feel? Was their experience in this game different from their experience in *Tug of War*? Were their feelings different? Why or why not?

Help them understand that when we work together we can work our way out of many conflicts. Then everyone wins! Enemies quickly become friends when we work together to solve a common problem.

Look at the following situations. Talk about how you might deal with them as **enemies** and **friends**. Help the children understand that cooperation and consideration of the other's feelings help solve problems.

Role-play these situations now or at another time:

Someone. . .   pushes you   cuts in line in front of you
                calls you a name   steps on your toes
                takes your pencil   accuses you of something unfairly

Jesus Says

Materials: Bible

Purpose: To reflect on Jesus' teaching about *friends* and *enemies*. To apply these teachings to daily situations of life.

Begin by playing a few minutes of the child's game *Simon Says*. Call the signals very quickly trying to get as many children as possible out. After a few rounds let SOME of the children who "messed up" back into the game.

Process the activity by discussing the following questions:
- How hard did you try to play the game?
- How did you feel when you messed up?
- How did you feel when you were let back into the game?
- How did you feel if you weren't let back into the game?

Ask the children "What would this game be like if it was called *Society Says*?" List some of the directions that society gives us to lead a good life. Examples: Get a good job. Live in a good neighborhood. Make lots of money. In Society's game do you get a second chance if you *mess up*?

Ask the children "What would this game be like if it was called *Jesus Says*?" List some of the directions that Jesus gives us about how to lead a good life. Use the Bible verses *Matthew 7:1–3, Luke 10:25–28, Matthew 5:43–44, Luke 6:27–31,* and *Matthew 7:12* to help the children. In Jesus' game do you get a second chance if you mess up?

Process the activity by discussing the following questions:
- Is it important to follow society's directions?
- Is it important to follow the directions Jesus gives?
- How are society's directions different from those of Jesus?
- Is it important that you get a second (or a third) chance to do it better?
- How does Jesus think "enemies" should act toward one another?
- How can we apply what we learn from Jesus to the situations in our life?

(Use some of the situations from the previous activity to give examples.)

If you did the *Friends and Enemies* activity, compare what you discovered there to your findings in the Bible by using these questions:
- How do the directions of Jesus apply to what you have learned about cooperation and resolving conflict?
- People aren't always going to agree. How do the directions given by Jesus help us work together?
- List some things that Jesus directs us to do when we are in conflict.

In the Driver's Seat   60 Minutes

Materials: *Steps to Peacemaking* poster. (p. 66) *Conflict Resolution Scenario Cards* (p. 71).

 Purpose: To learn and practice the *Steps to Peacemaking*.

Preparation: Cut out the Conflict Resolution Scenario Cards.

Play the child's game, *Red Light, Green Light*. Leave some large obstacles such as tables and chairs in the room for the children to go over, under or around as they come forward. Line the children up in the back of the room. Advise them that **the goal is to get everyone to the front of the room**. They should walk to the front of the room only when you call **Green Light** and turn your back to them. When you call **Red Light** they have to stop. You turn around quickly and if you see them move they have to go to the back of the room and start over. Play the game several times reminding them of the goal to get everyone to the front of the room.

Process the activity by discussing the following questions:
- How did you feel when playing the game?
- Did you compete with others or cooperate with them?
- What was the purpose of the game? Was it for one to win or all to succeed?
- Did your understanding of the purpose effect the way you played the game?
- Who was in control (In the driver's seat) of what you did to get to the front?
- Can we choose how we will respond to life situations in a similar way?

If you did the activity *Jesus Says* start with the list you made of things that Jesus directs us to do when we are in conflict. Ask if there are some rules that could be made to make it easier to cooperate and be Peacemakers. List their ideas.

Take out the *Steps to Peacemaking* poster. Ask, "Do any of our suggestions match the steps?" Go over the steps to be sure they understand them. Practice using them in a situation of your choice.

Allow the children to choose partners. Pass out the *Conflict Resolution Scenario* cards. Give them about five minutes to discuss and practice how they could use the *Steps to Peacemaking* to resolve the situation.

Present the role-plays remembering to stop them occasionally to point out the steps and involve the group in the process. After each role-play, summarize and invite comments from the group.

Process the activity by discussing the following questions:
- How easy was it to come up with ways to resolve the conflict?
- Were there any situations that could not be resolved? Why?
- How does following the Steps for Peacemaking put you in the driver's seat?

Conflict Resolution Scenario Cards

Two neighbors are arguing about who has to clean up the alley between their homes.	Your brother borrowed your bike. Now it has a flat tire.
Isabel is new in class. She speaks very little English and is often confused in class. She gets further behind in her work every day.	You and your friends always sit at the same lunch table. Today you see two bigger boys sitting there.
You do your math homework while at Joe's house. The next day he gives you your paper and says, "here, you left this at my house last night." When the papers are returned you see that his paper has the same answers as yours.	Two of your friends started fighting at a football game.
You are watching TV. It is time for your sister's favorite program so she changes the channel.	The game is almost over. You get mad because you think another player is cheating.
Someone called you a name.	Your parents just don't understand, you really need your own phone.

Stormy Weather

Materials: Newsprint and marker, *Conflict* (p. 73)and *Escalating Conflict* posters (p. 74), TV/VCR and video, *Harriet the Spy*, from Paramount.

Purpose: To examine the dynamics of conflict.

Ask the children, "In a perfect world do you think there would ever be conflict?" Let the children answer and, if necessary, point out that conflict is a natural occurrence between people. Like anger it has good points and bad points. Let the children name as many points as they can. Record them on the newsprint under the headings **Positive** and **Negative.** *(Conflict helps us see other points of view. Conflict can lead to growth and change. On the other hand, conflict can restrict progress, hamper relationships and even lead to violence.)*

Display the *Conflict* poster. Discuss the definition and causes of conflict. Ask the children if they can give examples of the causes.

Explain that when a conflict goes from bad to worse, we call it **escalation**. Display the *Escalating Conflict* poster. Discuss the differences between **showers**, **storms** and **typhoons**.

Introduce the video, *Harriet the Spy*. Tell the children to watch for the conflict in this movie. When and how does it escalate? What happens to resolve it? Show the video.

Process the activity by discussing the following questions:

• What caused the conflict to move from **showers** to **storm** to **typhoon**? What might have prevented escalation in each case?

• What might have happened if Harriet had spoken honestly to her parents when: 1) the journal was first read out loud? 2) the kids called her smelly? and 3) her parents took the notebook away?

• How does getting revenge affect the situation? What did Harriet gain by purposely hurting her friends? Is revenge really *sweet*?

• What help did Harriet finally get? Who are five people in your life to whom you can turn for help in a crisis?

• In the end, what turned things around? Why did the kids vote for Harriet for editor?

Conflict

Conflict is a clashing disagreement between opposing groups or individuals where:

- two or more parties want sole ownership of the same thing

- two or more parties can't agree on a common idea or plan of action

- one party's actions hurt another

Conflict is most often caused by:

- people seeing the same thing in different ways

- people expecting too much or too little or something different than they actually get

- people having different values

- people not getting their needs met

Escalating Conflict

TYPHOON

This is a conflict that has become out of control and dangerous. There may be feelings of fear, loneliness, helplessness and hopelessness. There seems to be no end in sight. There is a critical need for mediation and protection.

STORM

This involves a more serious offense and stronger feelings. There may be a loss of trust. It is longer lasting and might need a third party to mediate.

SHOWER

This is an annoyance resulting in mild feelings. It usually lasts a short time and can be easily settled without help.

Journaling

Materials: *Peacemaker's Journal* and pens.

Purpose: Quiet journaling time helps each child reflect on the personal meaning of each lesson.

During your time with the children encourage them to reflect and journal on any of the following ideas:

- Design a T-shirt with a slogan for the kids in *Harriet the Spy*.
- Was there ever a time when someone you thought was an enemy turned out to be a friend? Write about it.
- When Jesus sees how we treat one another at (school, camp, etc.), He might say, " _____ ."

STEPPING OUT AS A PEACEMAKER

Too often children's TV programing teaches violent ways to handle conflict. Research children's TV programs over a one month period to see which ones teach positive ways to handle conflict. Which ones show violence or other negative ways to handle conflict? Mount a letter writing campaign to producers, sponsors and newspaper editors encouraging better programing. Demand that violent programing be taken off the air.

Index of Activities

Index of Posters and Worksheets